The Psychology of Sailing
the sea's effects on mind and body

The Psychology of Sailing
the sea's effects on mind and body

Professor Michael Stadler
Translated by Sally A. R. Bates MA

International Marine Publishing Company
Camden, Maine

First published in 1987 in Great Britain
by Adlard Coles
William Collins Son & Co
8 Grafton Street
London W1X 3LA

Published by International Marine Publishing Co, a division of Highmark
Publishing Ltd, 21 Elm Street, Camden, Maine 04843

Printed and bound in Great Britain

10 9 8 7 6 5 4 3 2 1

Library of Congress Cataloging-in-Publication Data

Stadler, Michael, 1941–
    Psychology of sailing.

    Bibliography: p.
    Includes index.
    1. Sailing—Psychological aspects.   I. Title.
GV811.7.P75S7 1988   797.1'24'019   87–21375
ISBN 0–87742–963–4

Contents

Foreword   vii

Introduction – Sailing with mind and body   *1*

1 Where your senses let you down – Sensory performance and
   sensory illusions at sea   *4*
- *How does the world get into your head?*
- *We can get used to anything – on the ability of our sensory organs
  to adapt to the surrounding conditions*
- *Straight ahead without a compass – how we orientate ourselves in
  the horizontal plane*
- *Buoys are magnetic – characteristics of figure and ground*
- *How far and how big? – visual evaluation of size and distance*
    In good visibility
    At night and in fog
- *The 'moon illusion' and other optical illusions*
    The ominous wall of cloud
    Will the boat fit this space?
    Which is the heavier?
- *Where is the whistle buoy? – perception of the direction and
  distance of sound sources*
- *Which is the right horizon? – contrast, irradiation, equalisation*
- *The colourful world of sailing – a little on colour perception*
- *What is moving, what isn't moving? – perceived motion is relative*
    The moving navigational light – auto-kinetic phenomena
    Jumping lights – stroboscopic movement
    The wandering moon – induced movement
- *Attention and strain in prolonged observation – lookout and radar*

- *Relative movements on the goggle-box – problems of radar interpretation*
- *How to identify a navigational light without a stopwatch – the perception and estimation of time*

2 The psychological factors in seasickness   57
- *Anyone can become seasick*
- *Can seasickness be avoided without medicine?*
- *The frequency, symptoms and course of seasickness*
- *Which way up, which way down? – perception of the vertical*
- *What causes seasickness?*
- *The fear of illness is enough to make us ill*
- *What can we do about seasickness?*
- *When we have acquired our sea-legs*
- *Some advice in summing up*

3 Recreational sailing as hard work   75
- *Considerations of work psychology in a leisure sport*
- *Everyone has a job to do but no-one is satisfied – dos and don'ts in the division of labour on board*
- *On watch*
- *Initial shock – reaction or reflection?*
- *Safety at sea – not merely a question of technology but also of awareness*

4 The crew as a social group – Socio-psychology on small vessels   91
- *The psychological situation at sea*
- *The* Apollonia *case*
- *Social distancing – the problems of living space on board*
- *Social isolation at sea*
- *The oceans are free – but we make territorial claims upon them*
- *Group-dynamics on board*
- *What gives the skipper his authority? – on the socio-psychology of ship leadership*
- *So much frustration – and then aggression*

5 What drives us at sea? – A word on the motivation of the sailor   115
- *The sailor and anxiety – producing action or immobility?*
- *Why do yachtsmen insist time and again on risking danger at sea?*

Index   119

Foreword

One will not find the psychological aspects of sailing dealt with anywhere in yachting literature. Yet on board a yacht they are omnipresent, and in many more manifestations than one would commonly suppose. The reader will soon discover how fascinating this area is. Many phenomena which are very familiar but which previously have remained unexplained will suddenly become intelligible. The group-dynamic problems and social tensions that can arise from living together in cramped conditions have a psychological as well as a physical cause. If one recognises this fact the problems can be solved or circumvented – for example, through more sensible divisions of labour or an alternative organisation of the watches. There is also an extensive chapter on seasickness.

Instead of taking the daily experience of the sailor as a starting point, I have attempted to introduce individual problems systematically. Each chapter, therefore, stands on its own although the structure of the book follows the inherent logic of the psychological theme – from fundamental perceptual phenomena to the problems of co-existence on board.

Anyone wishing to extend their knowledge will find a bibliography at the end of the book. This lists various publications from the different specialist areas which I have drawn upon in my text.

This book would not have been possible without the inspiration afforded in passing by those with whom I have sailed. I dedicate this book to them.

I am especially indebted to my friends and sailing companions who have read the individual chapters and given me much encouragement and advice: Dr. Christian Funke, Dr. Heinz Offe, Kpt. Jochen

Schmellenkamp, Dr. Peter Schwab and Dr. Theo Wehner.

I received particular motivation from Frau Margot Eikermann who typed the manuscript twice without losing her interest in the subject.

Prof. Dr. Michael Stadler
Bremen, 1984

Introduction:
Sailing with mind and body

Only a few years ago a book about psychology at sea would have caused most yachtsmen to shake their heads in disbelief. Navigation, new technology, meteorology, maritime law, boat design and construction, indeed even medicine, are specialist subjects which anyone who takes to the water must deal with sooner or later, but psychology? How does a subject foremostly associated with the psychiatrist's couch and 'mental striptease' become relevant at sea, where one is surely concerned with more tangible matters? Conceivably, perhaps, it plays a part in the tactical machinations of competition, as in a race. However, a manual specifically for this latter kind of psychology cannot be written, for so much depends upon the special nature of each situation and on the individual's response to the moment. But there are other facts about modern-day boating that deserve consideration. In recent years the human element has been taken into account more and more in the design and construction of sea-going vessels. Previously there was a prevailing tendency among boatbuilders and yachtsmen to entrust the ship's safety to technological factors above all, and to blame 'human error' for accidents without taking the suitability of the technical equipment for human use into account. The problems of leadership on board are also being discussed more often these days. Reports of long-distance voyages and offshore races are dealing more frequently with the psychological and group dynamic problems encountered by the relatively unprepared crew-members. One impressive example of this is the report of *Walrus III* in the Whitbread round the world race. Furthermore, the inexplicable experiences of many sailors during night watches may have already served to arouse interest in psychological phenomena.

We sail with mind and body, which is to say we do not function on a boat in a purely physical capacity, rather life at sea affects the entire being, behaviour and personality. Mind and body form an inseparable whole. Our physical state affects our behaviour and perception just as our behaviour and perception influence our physical state. The best example of this is seasickness, which has interacting physical and psychological components. It is not possible to convey knowledge of psychology at sea in the manner of a recipe book – one cannot draw up a psychological first-aid manual – but rather insight is afforded primarily through personal association with psychological phenomena and problems. The recognition of the psychological elements or the psychological patterns involved in a particular situation render it at once easier to manipulate, control or alter.

The objective of this book is to facilitate the reader's recognition of the psychological and socio-psychological phenomena which he encounters at sea, and thus to enhance his ability to cope with them. He may learn to foresee possible misinterpretations of sensory data as well as group dynamic tensions, and hence be better prepared to bring these under control. Many readers may succeed in gaining a greater feeling for social interactions at sea.

Some yachtsmen clearly believe that perceptual problems and human error can be eliminated permanently by the new resources offered by modern navigational devices, thereby ensuring optimal safety levels at sea. The problems of radar observation exemplified in this book, however, show that technical navigation merely translates psychological problems into another medium where they reappear in a more serious form.

One final point to demonstrate the importance of ocean-going psychology concerns the role that the sea can play in the development of the self, the individual personality. The educational value of seafaring has been preached to us by our forefathers since time immemorial. But what is really meant by this? How can living, crammed together with others in the most confined space, under adverse and dangerous conditions, with no possibility of escape, make a worthwhile contribution to character formation? The answer to this question brings to light contradictory evidence. On the one hand, the sea-going environment, life in a 'microcosm', is damaging to the health. According to a recent study 12 per cent of all seamen suffer from neurotic illnesses – this is clearly more than in other occupational groups. On the other hand, the endeavours and results of educational and therapeutic youth sailing organisations indicate that life at sea has remarkable positive effects on maladjusted, educationally backward, wayward or delinquent youngsters: the activities of finding one's identity, gaining self-confidence, learning diverse skills and working of necessity as part of a team engaged in a common activity and sharing a common goal – and still managing to hold one's own – show that a ship provides a remarkably beneficient environment for character building.

1   *Where your senses let you down*

Sensory performance and sensory illusions at sea

How does the world get into your head?

Our ability to see stars thousands of light years away, smell a few molecules of a chemical substance in a cubic centimetre of air, distinguish time differences in very weak sound waves down to 1/2000th of a second, or discern deviations of mast halyards from the vertical of less than one degree, depends on a complicated interplay of physical, physiological and psychological factors. We tend to think that we perceive the world about us through our sensory organs (for instance our eyes) as if we are looking at it through a window. In reality exactly the opposite is true. We receive external stimuli (light and sound waves) through the sensory organs and these are carried by the nervous system to the brain where, in conjunction with earlier experiences stored in the memory, they are co-ordinated to form a picture of our surroundings. We do not, however, reproduce the outside world in every detail, rather we see, hear, and so on, only that which is new or unexpected or what is important for orientation. In selecting from the innumerable stimuli arriving at the brain, errors in perception can clearly occur. Only by focusing the attention on specific details of the environment, in other words, by really looking and really listening, can our perceptions reach a high degree of accuracy.

Our perceptions are not to be equated with a technically reproduced image of the world. What we see with our eyes (or better, our visual system) is considerably superior to the highest quality photographic reproduction. For example, let us compare the visual experience of the actual course of a race with its photographic (or filmed) counterpart. While we are able to follow visually the thrilling rivalry of two yachts, at a certain distance a photograph or film can only offer us white (moving) dots. Researchers in perception speak here of 'Constancy Phenomena'. Things appear to us to retain their size regardless of their distance, their colour and brightness regardless of their illumination, and their spatial position and orientation regardless of the observer's relative position and movements. The disadvantage, however, of such 'improvements' on the visual image by Constancy Phenomena is that under extreme conditions they can give rise to inconsistencies and illusions which are particularly invidious at sea.

If we speak frequently in this chapter of the 'laws of perception', it is because there are certain stimuli which all human beings, whatever their cultural or environmental conditions, interpret in a similar way. The stellar constellations may serve as an example of this. The measuring instruments used by astronomers can locate objects of differing brightness and physio-chemical properties throughout the firmament. The grouping of these points of light into specific constellations which we think of (and see!) as being linked to one another by direct connecting lines, is another psychological phenomenon. Be that as it may, the arrangement of these connecting lines is not a matter of choice, rather the grouping of stars to form constellations obeys quite specific and accurately researched formal principles, which are generally valid in the field of visual perception. To combine the stars in The Plough (Big Dipper) in the manner depicted in Figure 1a offends our laws of perception so much that the old familiar constellation is distorted beyond all recognition. In nearly every civilisation of the world, then, the stars are perceived as being grouped as in Figure 1c, even though they are given different names and attributed different meanings. The same applies to Orion and the other constellations.

Such general rules, however, should not hide the fact that perception is also influenced by cultural and individual differences. We should remember that perception is not a function which follows a fixed pattern from birth on, but rather develops, refines and improves itself in the course of one's life and in accordance with one's lifestyle. Correct and accurate perception may be learnt. Many a yachtsman might recall, as a newcomer to the sport, looking helplessly at the rigging of ships and boats and being confused by the multitude of lines, blocks and topmasts. In time he came to know their function, to distinguish between them, and so increase his understanding of the sailing rig. It could be said that the experienced sailor perceives more than the beginner, even though both receive the same sensory data.

All our sensory organs work together to give an integral impression of the objects and signs in our environment. Thus we perceive the wind simultaneously through our various sense organs: visually when we look at the anemometer or the sails, and acoustically when we hear it whistling through the shrouds and stays: but we also feel

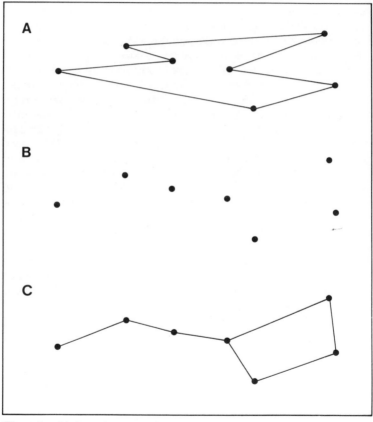

Figure 1.   (a) An unknown constellation? (B) the stars of the plough (Big Dipper) which are universally recognised in the configuration shown in (C).

the touch of the wind on the skin and the cold due to the greater conductivity of the mass of air, while the muscular and spatial sense as well as the sense of balance tell us that the body must be held at an angle in order to maintain its upright position against the wind. Many sailors even claim they can smell it! It is only by the co-operation of our sensory organs, then, that we are granted a comprehensive picture of the diverse elements of the physical world, and we are thus enabled to modify our actions appropriately.

Some general characteristics common to all our sensory organs should receive a brief mention: in relaying stimuli, each of the senses has both a high and a low pain threshold. There are, for example, sounds so soft that we cannot hear them, and others so loud that they are cut off before they break the pain barrier. The movement of the minute hand on a watch exists objectively without doubt, as we discover through repeated examination, but we cannot 'see' it – it is subliminal. We see only a little of the movement of the blades of a fan at high speed, since it is outside of the temporal resolution capacity of our eyes – this is supraliminal. In some people these thresholds are dependent on the adaptability of the sensory organs, in others, however, they also depend on the physical condition of the organs, or on the age or 'sensitivity' of the individual. Thus at sea it is often found that an order shouted against the wind will be understood by one member of the crew and not heard by another; or that some can make out a distant flare quite clearly before others can see it at all; or that one person can smell the food burning while others remain in unimpaired anticipation of the meal, and so on.

At sea – an environment which is foreign, unpredictable and dangerous to man – our sensory organs must operate completely and with total efficiency as a prerequisite for true appreciation of the situation and correspondingly suitable action. That is why anyone taking command of a ship must first have their most important senses (sight and hearing) tested.

We can get used to anything – on the ability of our sensory organs to adapt to the surrounding conditions

The human organism has many different ways of adapting itself to prevailing environmental conditions. This is particularly true of the sensory organs. We all know for instance how our eyes become accustomed to the dark, so that moments after stepping into the open at night we are able to distinguish details where before all was black. This is why, when sailing at night, we should try to avoid having deck lighting on, or to have light shining from below into the cockpit, so that the helmsman has optimal opportunity to adapt to the surrounding darkness. When we step back into bright light we are dazzled at first, but within just a few seconds, we readjust to the new lighting conditions. By regulating the average intake of light through an involuntary contraction and dilation of the pupils, the eyes simultaneously increase our capacity for discrimination within the parameters of the prevailing conditions.

A similar process of adaptation occurs in the middle colour range of our field of vision. If, for example, we put on sunglasses with green lenses, we at first see our surroundings in a green light. Red colours are considerably toned down in the process. Given time to adapt, however, the visual system locates a new zero point on the red-green spectrum as it makes allowances for the green filter of the sunglasses, with the result that the red-green distribution in the environment is once again normal.

Adaption processes generally serve to make an organism sensitive to new and unexpected stimuli, while the uniform, familiar, ever recurring stimuli recede to the back of the attention in time.

The drawback to such processes of adaption is that there is generally a negative, (that is, opposite or reverse) after-effect which occurs when the uniform stimulation decreases. For instance, if we look down for any length of time at the water parting under the prow, this uniform stimulation will imperceptibly diminish our eyes' impression of the water's movement. We become fully aware of this only once we return our attention to the deck. Objects which are securely fixed in place suddenly seem to be moving irresistably upwards; although in reality they are quite motionless. In psychology this after-sensation of movement is known as the 'waterfall illusion'.

Straight ahead without a compass – how we orientate ourselves in the horizontal plane

In contrast to the sensory capacity of many animals, man is not equipped with special organs to facilitate his orientation in uniform surroundings such as the desert, modern cities and the sea. Research on bird flight has shown that birds may have an inbuilt biological sun, star and magnetic compass, and possibly even an inertia navigation system. This would explain how they accomplish their amazing annual migrations, and how they are able to find their way home from any point of release (witness the behaviour of homing pigeons!). In place of such biological equipment man possesses a high aptitude for learning and a high degree of inventiveness. The rudiments of astronomical navigation were already developed by the time the very first seafarers dared sail the open seas, and the magnetic compass had already been invented some 3000 years ago. In conditions of bad visibility – cloud or fog – and in the absence or failure of a magnetic compass, the human capacity for orientation is, however, sadly lacking.

The term 'geographical orientation' is generally understood to cover three different activities:

(1) maintaining a predetermined route once underway,
(2) finding a particular direction,
(3) orientating ourselves in a particular territory by our spatial sense.

The latter activity also includes the ability to read maps and charts, to construct such aids, and to develop a so called 'cognitive map' of a familiar region – a basis for orientation which exists only in the mind.

(1) It is well-known that people move in a circle when they are cut off from sensory information about their surroundings (as for example in fog). In most cases this circular motion is clockwise and occurs whether one is walking, swimming, driving a car or steering a yacht. Physical asymmetry (right-handedness) is often thought to be the cause of this, although the Coriolis force with which the yachtsman will already be familiar for its effect on wind direction is another factor to consider. The circular motions are in general so slow that they remain subliminal to the rotary motion sensors in the organs of balance. An inborn asymmetry of the latter is far more likely to be the cause of this behaviour. Anyone who has ever been dinghy sailing on an inland lake and suddenly been surprised by fog will appreciate how difficult it is to reach the bank by simply steering straight ahead. If there is wind, which there generally is not, one can orientate oneself by a particular setting of the sail or by keeping an eye on the burgee.

Out on the open sea, when becalmed or in fog, orientation is possible through observation of the swell. Here the sense of motion (of balance and position) play a greater part than sight. Sailing head on into the waves produces a recognizable pitching motion, while side on produces a little pitching. Thus for every course at a diagonal to the swell there is a particular pattern of pitch and roll in the boat's movement.

Changes in the situation through changes in wind direction, and above all in the tidal stream, must be taken into consideration here. If we concentrate, our motion sensors are able to detect any change in the pattern of rolling and pitching. The sailors of the South Pacific were able to navigate quite accurately by observing the waves in this way.

In fog when we have neither wind nor waves to help in plotting a straight course, and when it is not even possible to see the wake, the only thing left is to break out a line (a logline or fishing line) with a small drag anchor. This line should be attached to the mast and allowed to run out over the stern. The helmsman can then steer by keeping it exactly in line with the keel.

(2) The best clues in determining a particular direction in foreign surroundings are provided by the stars. From early on mankind adopted many different methods of astronomical navigation. Even without any previous knowledge or special training most people are able to orient themselves roughly, on land or sea, by the position of the sun. The main points of the compass can also be identified simply on the basis of the wind directions which are typical in certain weather conditions. However when there are no visual clues, as is the case in conditions of bad visibility and fog, then the human capacity for spatial orientation is extremely poor compared with that of many other animals. In its place man has his greater intelligence – enough perhaps to construct a makeshift compass in times of real emergency.

(3) The capacity for spatial imagination – the ability to depart from the egocentric view with the 'I' at the centre and to adopt different spatial perspectives – is a central component of human intelligence and is one of the things which is measured in IQ tests. The yachtsman is often called upon to exercise this facility. In a skerry region, for example, in the cockpit of his boat he has an eye-level perspective of approximately two metres. If he goes below deck to his navigation table and looks at his charts he acquires a birds-eye view. Without a second thought he turns the surrounding world about in his imagination since the north point on his chart as it lies on the chart

table is not necessarily in alignment with the north point as shown on the ship's compass. Here the skipper is required to construct a 'cognitive map' in which he has a certain degree of mental freedom and the perspective of which he can alter in a matter of seconds.

Only beginners are likely to have difficulties steering a craft by compass. Things are not made easier by the fact that there are various types of compass and compass displays. If the lubber line is at the front of the compass the helmsman must turn the rudder in the direction of the desired course, while if the line is aft, the rudder should be turned in the opposite direction. Problems arise chiefly because it is so difficult for us to accept the fact that the compass card is virtually stationary and directionally stable while the boat turns about it. This is because when there are two parts moving against each other (here the boat and the compass card) we generally perceive the enclosed part to be mobile and the surrounding part to be stationary. This phenomenon is explained more fully later in the book (p.39). Mechanical knowledge of the operation of the rudder is of little help to beginners since, in an emergency – when it is important to respond quickly and correctly – their immediate reaction is to turn and go in the opposite direction – although in so doing they may perhaps cause an accidental jibe or collision. In time, they learn to construct a spatial frame of reference in which the compass rose and the earth's surface (the seabed) are stable and in which the boat, waves and navigator's perspective are mobile. As experience shows, however, not everyone achieves this with the same degree of success.

Buoys are magnetic – characteristics of figure and ground

An experienced skipper I know used to say that buoys are 'magnetic' whenever he wished to point out the dangers of sailing in a buoyed channel with an inexperienced man at the helm. Indeed inexperienced crew members often find that a buoy they have had fixed in their sights for some time, and which they have intended to leave well to starboard will suddenly, when almost reached, be very close to starboard, just as if the boat were being irresistably drawn towards it. To make matters worse, a wind at 60° to the head always seems to pick up in such situations, so that the helmsman is not able to sail any closer to the wind in order to avoid collision with the buoy. The best thing the skipper can do in these circumstances is order an emergency manoeuvre to starboard, passing the buoy close on the port beam.

What has gone wrong here? If the helmsman had been paying attention to the compass instead of keeping his sights fixed on the

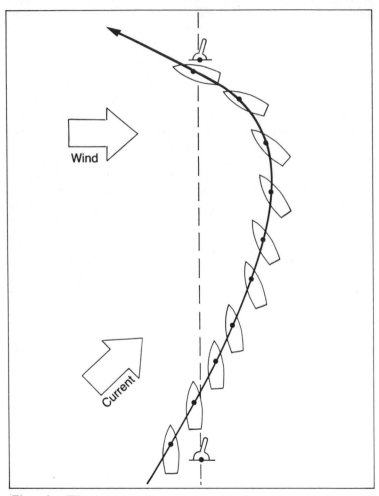

Figure 2.   What happens when one steers by the position of the buoy instead of keeping an eye on the compass.

buoy he would have noticed an initially imperceptible but ever stronger change in course to port. He has travelled a 'Dog Curve' (Fig 2). In order to clarify this term we must make an excursion into the evolutionary history of the vertebrate. Different animal species have in the course of their development adapted to suit different environmental conditions: on land, in the sea and in the air. Thus, while waterfowl are suited to life afloat, dogs, as land animals, will not venture into the water without a special reason. Similarly man, like most of the ape family, is not a swimmer by nature. Ducks, meanwhile, adopt the easiest and most energy conserving method of reaching their place of destination in a water flow and Figure 3 illustrates how, in order to reach a particular shelter on the other side of the river, they make allowances for the current by aligning their bodies in an upstream direction with the result that they cross the river at right angles and in the shortest way possible.

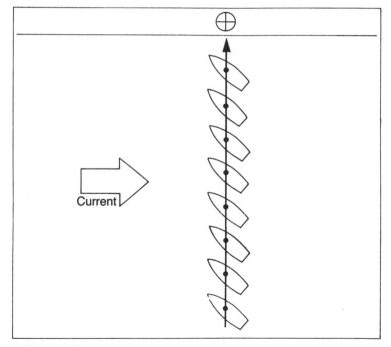

Figure 3.   The way a duck crosses a river.

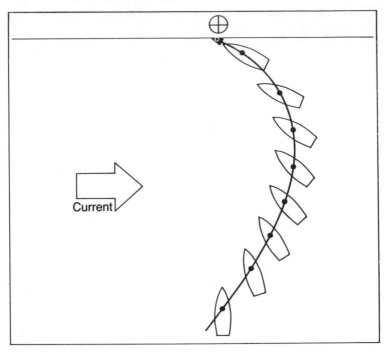

Figure 4.   The 'Dog Curve'.

The 'Dog Curve' is brought about quite differently (see Fig 4). In order to reach a particular point on the opposite bank a dog always aims directly for it and, as he is continually being displaced by the current, thus describes a parabolic curve. The dog behaves in a similar manner on land as he does in the water. For example, if he wishes to reach his master when the latter is travelling at an angle to him, he takes as little account of the independent movement of his object as he does of his own displacement by the current in the river.

That people behave in a similar manner on land and at sea is not primarily due to an inability to evaluate and make due allowance for the movement of the object or their own drift, but because it is difficult to orientate oneself in an empty space without an object to aim for. In most everyday situations people's actions are planned and goal-orientated. That is, we resolve to do something, fix upon a goal in our minds which is to be the outcome of our actions, and so organise our behaviour in order to achieve this goal in a more or less direct fashion. Psychologists postulate that our movements and actions are directly governed by these anticipated outcomes. When, however, we not only have the objective in our mind's eye but can also see it in front of us, then the influence of this 'real' goal on our behaviour is naturally all the more forceful. The preference of a goal object to empty space is supported by a psychological rule of perception.

Figure 5 is a well known demonstration of the 'figure-ground' relation. On initial viewing most people see a white goblet on a black background. After continued gazing, however, one notices that the

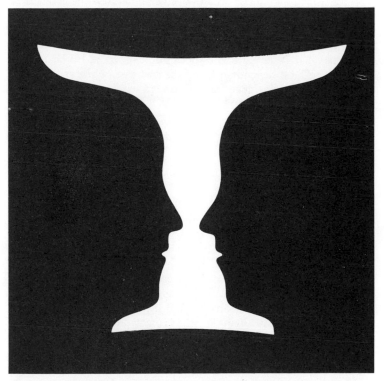

Figure 5. The figure-ground relation: only one image prevails, either the goblet or the profiles, while the other forms the background.

contours of the goblet also outline two black profiles facing each other. The white goblet is suddenly seen as the background. It is only possible to see one of the images at a time, either the goblet or the profiles, because the prevailing percept gives way to the alternate and becomes the background. Only the figure then is delineated, not the ground – this is unstructured and seems to spread out behind the object. Figures as discrete shapes in our field of vision will, therefore, always attract the attention while the ground, with nothing to hold the interest, lies unnoticed. This is why we find it so difficult to steer for a point in the distance at sea, where the background is particularly featureless. There is nothing to fix the helmsman's gaze as all points on the water surface and horizon look the same.

Sailing in a 'Dog Curve' in a buoyed channel must be avoided at all costs since the path of the boat, as Figure 2 demonstrates, can lead over shallows, even though the helmsman believes himself to have kept within the line of the buoys. The only way the inexperienced yachtsman can make sure this does not happen is by keeping a constant check on his course using the compass, while at the same time making due allowance for drift due to wind and tide.

How far and how big? – visual evaluation of size and distance

In good visibility

Our perceptions of the size and the distance of objects on land and at sea are inextricably linked. Figure 6 shows the physical-optical projectional relations of two objects on the retina of the eye. Lighthouse A is half as big and half as far away as Lighthouse B. Both however produce an image of the same size because of the concave shape of the retina. In everyday life these distortions of size and form pass completely unnoticed. Psychologists refer to this as 'size constancy'. It means that objects and living organisms when seen from a distance do not shrink in size as one would expect from their perspectival projection on a two-dimensional surface, but are (approximately) the same size as when viewed from a closer vantage point.

The following diagrams attempt to show why this is the case. The brain does not organise the information reproduced on the back of

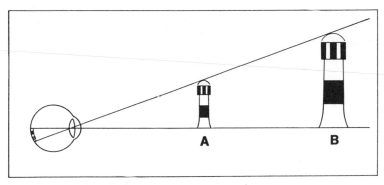

Figure 6. Optical projection on the retina: the images produced by objects A and B are the same size.

the eye two-dimensionally, but rather we always see the depth of space as well, and make overall allowances for the position objects occupy in space. Ashore or at sea, we always see a surface stretching before us into the distance which has a texture comprising elements of approximately the same size (see Fig. 7). These elements can be any of a diverse range of things: trees, houses, tufts of grass, clods of earth, ripples on the surface of the water, streaks of surf, waves and so on. The further away they are from the standpoint of the observer the smaller and denser they become until they almost completely merge on the horizon.

As in Figure 8, these texture-gradients can be represented simply by lines of increasing density. This produces a strong impression of spatial depth. The size of the vessels is not assessed according to their corresponding projectional relationships (their geometrical size in the diagram) but on the basis of their classification within the texture-gradients of the surface of the water. Thus the hull of Motorboat A is geometrically just as big as the hull of Freighter C. Motorboat A, however, only covers two elements (lines) of the texture-gradient while Freighter C, to the bilge alone, covers five. We therefore perceive Freighter C, both in the diagram and in reality, to be considerably larger than Motorboat A but, at the same time, considerably further away as well. If we now compare Motorboat A with Motorboat B it appears that B is geometrically much smaller than A but, like A, it also covers two texture lines. Because the same fixed relationship exists between boat A and its

Figure 7.   Spatial depth as determined by texture-gradients.

texture-gradient and between boat B and its texture gradient, we perceive both to be about the same size but judge B to be further away. It is noteworthy that in the diagram the three letters A, B, C appear to have been taken from the same case (in other words, they look the same size).

The increasing density of the texture-gradients at sea is often misinterpreted by sailors when they are becalmed. The hope that a little wind might yet rise leads them to believe that a little further on, where the texture gradient of the surface of the water is relatively

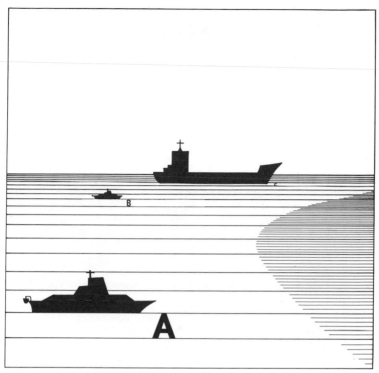

Figure 8. Judgement of the size of vessels at sea: within the texture-gradient Freighter (C) appears much larger than Motorboat (A) which is seen to be the same size as Motorboat (B).

dense, there is perhaps a little more wind than at the present position, where the surface is barely ruffled. In happy anticipation of catching up with the gentle breeze just two nautical miles away, the yachtsmen then starts up his engine only to find on arrival, and to his disappointment, that he has been the victim of an optical illusion. A change in the wind conditions within a particular area at sea, as can happen with a sudden squall or in the lee of a headland (see Fig. 9), would appear as an intensification of the texture gradients. These alterations tend, as a rule, to be plainly recognisable when the change in the gradients is abrupt.

The capacity of the visual system to evaluate size and distance by relating objects to each other within the texture-gradients, and to the texture-gradient itself, is amazingly accurate. Experiments have shown that the size and distance of objects in uniform gradients, such as expansive fields or the sea, can be assessed accurately if subjects

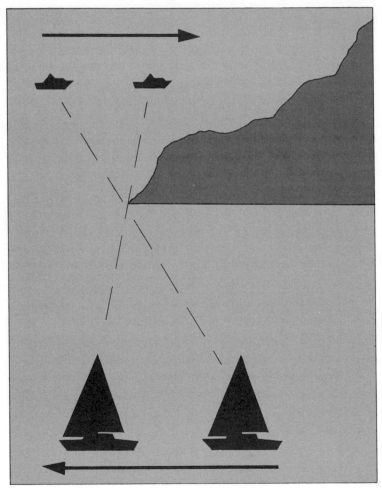

Figure 9.   From the sailor's perspective the motorboat does not appear to have moved. This makes it harder for him to judge its distance.

are aware of their objective relationships. Objects which are further away, therefore, may become less distinct but not necessarily smaller even if they are little more than a collection of dots on the retina.

A useful clue in judging the distance (and therefore also the size) of another vessel is spatial displacement within the visual field. A motorboat travelling at a speed of eight knots passes through more of the field of vision when it is nearby than when it is far away. However, due allowance must be made for the movement of one's own craft. If there is a fixed point between the vessels, a buoy or an outcrop of land for instance, then the displacement can be completely cancelled out (Fig. 9), making the judgement of size and distance uncertain.

At night and in fog

The perception of size and distance is made considerably more difficult and often quite impossible when there are no texture-gradients. There are essentially two circumstances where this is the case: when the object is not directly above the horizon (as with birds, aeroplanes, clouds and stars), and in conditions of reduced visibility (fog or darkness). It is true that the relationship between the perceived size and distance always remains more or less constant, that is, the further away an object is seen to be, the larger it must be, but in the absence of any clue to size and distance any number of interpretations is theoretically possible.

Thus in the aforementioned conditions gross errors of judgement frequently occur, and furthermore they differ greatly from person to person. This explains how the silhouette of an aircraft can just as easily be taken for a 10m long private jet flying at a height of 1000m as for a 40m long airliner flying at 4000m. An additional clue here, which may still make a realistic appraisal possible, is the speed of the aircraft. In order to have the same angular velocity the 4000m plane would have to be flying four times as fast as the plane at 1000m. Errors in the evaluation of the size and distance of clouds and heavenly bodies are discussed in the following section.

There have been investigations into the judgement of size and distance in fog which are of significance to the yachtsman. It has been found that with visibility between 30m and 130m objects seem to be roughly twice as far away (and thus also twice as large) as in clear weather. Figure 10 can convey only a very weak approximation of

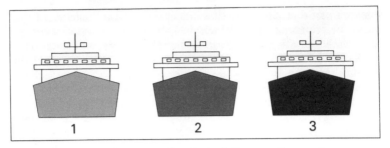

Figure 10.   The judgement of the size and distance of a vessel are dependent on contrast (clarity): Vessel (1) appears to be further away and thus larger than vessels (2) and (3).

this phenomenon. In such visibility illusions regarding the speed of other vessels can also occur, especially if they are approaching head-on. This is because when a boat is first sighted in these conditions it is judged to be considerably further away than it actually is, and so the distance it covers in the time it takes to approach is effectively doubled. The speed of approach is thus similarly overestimated.

It is generally regarded as a rule of perception that the lesser degree of contrast there is between the object and its background, the further away the object is. Photographers and artists call this effect 'atmospheric perspective' since even in clear weather more distant objects always appear to be less well defined than closer objects. In reduced visibility at sea this illusion is highly significant since many accidents and collisions are put down to the fact that headlands, lighthouse or other vessels were seen to be further away than they really were. Movement parallax can also be a valuable clue in judging distance: vessels or headlands moving slowly are further away than those moving quickly.

Points of light in the dark, such as position lights, illuminated buoys or navigational lights, prove an exception. Just as with fixed stars and planets, for whose actual size and distance we have no clues at all, the distance of lights at sea cannot be judged with any degree of accuracy; and this is particularly difficult in good visibility. Points of light alter their size so slightly as we approach that we cannot perceive the changes. Any increase in brightness also tends to remain below the threshold of our perceptions. Sailors must, therefore, be extremely careful at night when rounding a headland with offshore shallows while relying on visual judgements of the distance of the relevant navigational light. When the light is visibly closer, the craft is in immediate danger of running aground. The best way for a sailor to test this phenomenon is by aiming one night for a buoy which should be held more or less dead on course and which – because there is no movement parallax – can therefore give no clues as to how far away it is. The distance of the buoy does not seem to change for a long time even if it is approached at a good speed. All of a sudden, however, it is directly ahead and perilously close.

The 'moon illusion' and other optical illusions

A well-known phenomenon, one which will certainly be familiar to all those who sail and which has caused many a celestial navigator headaches in the past, is the 'moon illusion'. If one sees the moon directly above the horizon it appears considerably larger than when it is higher in the sky. The same applies to the sun: before it sets and after it rises it seems much bigger than when it is at its highest point above the horizon. If we measure the diameter of the sun with a sextant at different times of the year we only find differences of 1' at the most between summer and winter. In winter, at the point in its orbit when the earth is nearest the sun (the perihelion) the diameter of the sun measures 32.6'. In summer, when the earth is at its greatest distance from the sun (the aphelion), the diameter of the sun measures 31.6'. Likewise the diameter of the moon at its perigee measures 33.6' and, at its apogee, 29.4'. We do not find, however, similar differences in diameter corresponding to the height of the moon or sun – certainly not to the extent suggested by our perceptions. Both heavenly bodies appear about 50 per cent larger at the horizon (corresponding to about 15') than at the zenith. What we are dealing with here is a subjective phenomenon, the origination of which is explained below.

Most people do not see the sky above them as a hemisphere but as a flattened out arch (Fig. 11). If experimental subjects are asked to indicate the apparent middle point of the curve between the horizon and the zenith, the resultant angle β is 38° at the position of the observer as opposed to the expected angle of $\alpha = 45°$. The root of this phenomenon lies in the fact that we always perceive the highly organised surface between our standpoint (0) and the horizon (H) as

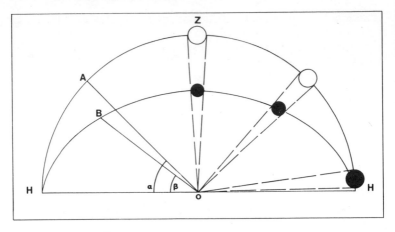

Figure 11.   The flattened out arch.

being longer than an empty textureless stretch of space – as for instance between the observation point (0) and the zenith (Z). If for once we ignore the slight differences in distance which occur due to the elliptical orbit of the moon (or sun), objectively the sun or moon is always the same distance from the observer whatever position it occupies in the sky. Subjectively, however, the planet (or star) is always seen to be orbiting along a flattened arch which means that at the horizon it is seen to be further away than when it is fully risen, or at the zenith. Size and distance are, however, as we have seen on page 16, so bound up with each other because of the way in which the eyes function that objects which possess the same visual angle but which are at a greater distance are considered to be larger. Figure 11 clearly shows how the object orbiting the flattened arch must increase in size as it nears the horizon.

A further geometric-optical illusion regarding the sun and moon has yet to be mentioned: Figure 12 is a demonstration of something that is much more plainly observed in reality; namely that, behind a bank of cloud, the sun no longer appears as a sphere but as a vertical ellipse. This happens because, in our perception, all angles which deviate from the right angle (90°) (here the four angles between the edge of the sun and the strips of cloud) appear increased. This is made clearer in Figure 13.

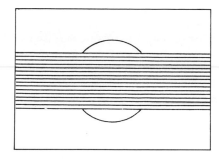

Figure 12. Behind the strips of cloud the sun no longer appears spherical but as a vertical ellipse.

Here we also see the angle of the diagonal to the horizontal lines increased (or their compliment reduced) so that the diagonal line appears interrupted in a stair-like fashion although it is drawn as a continuous straight line, something that can be confirmed by means of a simple ruler. This apparent perceived increase comes about because the angles – which are perspectively distorted on the retina – must be 'rectified' in the brain so that a right angle is seen as a right angle when the position of the observer changes.

The ominous wall of cloud

We have seen that appreciation of the size of objects is dependent on their classification in a texture-gradient of the earth's surface.

Figure 13. The Poggendorf Illusion: try placing a ruler along the diagonal line.

Judgement of the size and distance of objects in the sky, be they balloons, aeroplanes or clouds, is, in contrast, extremely difficult since here there is no texture-gradient available. The sailor who keenly observes the weather and its developments will already have met the situation in which an ominous wall of cloud seems to build up ahead. On closer approach this turns out to be broken up cumulus. The cloud has not changed at all, it is the sailor's perspective which has altered. Figure 14 shows how this pheno-menon comes about. Since there are no clues for judging the distance of the clouds, and since there is also no way of knowing their size, all cumulus clouds are seen to be equidistant (represented by the dotted lines). This is why, as the diagram shows, they appear to pile up on top of each other and thus often look more menacing than they are in reality.

Will the boat fit this space?

Another common optical illusion which frequently causes us problems in manoeuvering craft consists of the tendency we have to

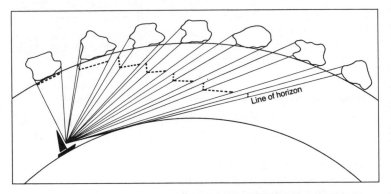

Figure 14.   The ominous wall of cloud: our judgement of the distance of the clouds corresponds to the dotted lines; this is why they seem to pile up above the horizon.

judge objects as generally being larger than empty spaces. So it is that we often worry whether the mast really will fit under the bridge ahead although we have already checked the clearance umpteen times in the handbook. We experience similar concern when the harbour master tries to guide us into a space on an already fully occupied pontoon. The gap seems far too small, but once we have attempted it, it proves to be quite adequate with 3m to spare fore and aft.

Which is the heavier: 1 kilo of feathers or 1 kilo of lead?

Reminiscent of this familiar children's riddle is an optical illusion to which adults, against their better judgement, also fall prey; the size-weight illusion. To the sense of touch, a large volume seems lighter than a small volume of objectively equal weight. Conversely however, our visual sense generally equates a larger volume with a greater mass and therefore also with a greater weight. This is why a keel boat on a trailer looks so unstable – because the point of gravity, due to the heavy ballast keel, appears much higher up to us than it really is. Similarly we perceive a ship travelling under ballast (in other words empty) as being considerably heavier, on account of its much greater visible volume, than a fully laden ship drawing more water because of its heavy cargo (see Fig 15). Illusions of this kind are due to the 'logic' which is peculiar to our perceptual systems. In everyday life we often have to counter this with world knowledge and our powers of reason.

These optical illusions originate, for the most part, in perceptual mechanisms which actually serve to reproduce our surroundings more effectively and more accurately – in other words more or less independently of the observer's changing perspective and relative distance from the objects of perception. Most of the optical illusions in daily life pass completely unnoticed since we are not in the habit

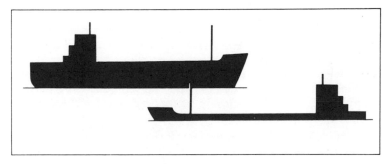

Figure 15. Which ship looks heavier?

of checking our perceptions off against reality with a ruler. However this means that optical illusions can be so forceful that, generally speaking, we have no defence against them. Knowledge of these perceptual mechanisms has been employed through the ages by architects and designers either to create an illusion or to compensate for expected illusions.

Where is the whistle buoy? – perception of the direction and distance of sound sources.

With our auditory apparatus we are able not only to perceive noises, music or language but also the distance and direction of the objects from which the sound comes. Thus hearing, just like the visual system, belongs among the 'distance senses' which convey information to us about the position of objects in surrounding space.

Sound emitting objects cause periodic changes in the density of the surrounding medium (for example air or water) which spread out spherically in all directions as the sound pressure waves which come in contact with the ears. The speed of the waves depends on the transmitting medium – 333m/s through air and 1,520m/s in water. In a vacuum, on the other hand, there is absolutely no sound transmission at all. Sine waves are distinguished by their frequency, amplitude and phase. Young people are able to distinguish different pitches in a frequency range from 20Hz to 20,000Hz. As we get older the higher frequencies become less discernible. The amplitude of the sound waves – the sound intensity – is perceived by us in terms of loudness.

All the noises and sounds in our environment are made up of multiple overlying sine waves, and each sound is a specific combination of low, middle and high frequencies whose characteristics are immediately recognisable. Pure sine waves with only one frequency do not exist in nature – nor can they be reproduced by musical instruments, but only artificially by tone generators. There are, in contrast, many noises which contain a very broad spectrum of almost all possible frequencies in random combinations. For example, the noise of the wind and water in stormy weather at sea. Such complex noises can of course also contain all the frequencies which constitute speech or music. It thus often happens that the sailor who has been exposed to this white noise for a long time, and who is also worn out from struggling against the storm, will succumb to the illusion that he is hearing voices or music even though he is quite alone. This is not a psycho-pathological symptom but an entirely normal occurrence which many people experience. Even in the normal environment our acoustic system (and this includes the nerves leading to the brain) operates a constant filtering process. This selects the frequencies which are of greater significance for survival from the background of noise, which might otherwise mask them. Without this filtering process we would not be able to understand what the crewmember calling out to us from the fo'c'sle was saying. In extreme cases, when one is tired and perhaps in a position where the sound of another voice would be welcome, it can quite easily happen that the acoustic system understands something from the stimuli which in reality does not exist.

At sea, especially in conditions of reduced visibility like fog, accurate appraisal of the direction and distance of a source of sound, such as a whistle buoy or another vessel's fog horn, is extremely important. Fog, which is air saturated with water particles, carries sound much better than dry air. Even the softest sounds penetrate it from a long way away. For this reason it is important to take the utmost care when trying to judge distance in such conditions.

Accurate perception of the distance of a sound source presupposes furthermore that one already has an idea of its loudness. The intensity of the sound diminishes by the square of the distance from the source, which means that a soft sound can either be coming from a source nearby which is transmitting softly or a source which is further away but transmitting more loudly. To achieve an accurate interpretation of the sensory data here one must gather all the information available from the other senses as well. Fortunately intensity is not the only criterion for judging the distance of sound sources. There is a further clue: with pure sine waves we have no capacity for judging distance at all, which proves that the frequency spectrum has an important part to play. Over longer distances through the air high frequencies are filtered out from the sound spectrum with the result that a more distant noise sounds dull and a nearer noise sound higher. Thunder is the obvious example here: nearby it produces a high, crashing sound while from a distance it seems dull and rumbling. Correspondingly a dull and soft whistle is more likely to indicate a transmitting vessel some distance away and a high, loud whistle may signal a potential collision close at hand.

The ability to judge the distance of a sound source accurately only comes with experience. It is, however, much easier to gauge the direction. In favourable conditions Azimuth variations of one degree can be discerned. In less favourable conditions, when trying to pinpoint simultaneously different sound sources at different angles, accuracy still comes within ten degrees. How do we account for the amazing performance of our auditory system? Essentially by the fact that it is structured as a double organ. If we assume that a sound source is located at an angle of 45 degrees to the direction the head is facing, one ear is orientated towards the source while the other is lying in the 'sound shadow'. This results in a difference in the intensity with which the sound waves reach the inner ear mechanisms in each ear. Since lower frequencies can go around the head while high frequencies are more likely to be reflected from the side of the head which is towards the sound source, perception of the difference in intensity between the ears is most effective with high frequency sounds.

The sound pressure waves meet each ear at slightly different times, and this time difference also plays a part in ensuring efficiency in locating the direction of the source. As previously mentioned, the speed of sound in air is 333 m/s. The distance between the ears measured through the head is 16cm. Therefore a sound coming at a right angle to the head would have to travel 16cm further in order to reach the ear in the sound shadow. This corresponds to a time difference of 1/2 ms (millisecond). If the sound occurs at an angle of 60 degrees to the head the auditory system still discerns time differences of up to 0.05 ms (in other words the twenty thousandth part of a second). Time differences can naturally only be perceived at the beginning, at the end or with each alteration in a sound. In order to facilitate the location of sounds which are uniform for several seconds at a time, the auditory system additionally distinguishes the phase differences between sound waves arriving at the ears. This phase shift (expressed as an angle) is a fixed and constant value which does, however, become inaccurate at high frequencies, where the phases recur quickly. Determination of the phase difference, therefore, serves principally to simplify the location of lower frequency (or lower pitch) sounds.

A problem exists, however, in the fact that for all three indicators mentioned above, that is, for each difference in intensity, time and phase there are a whole series of points in the space surrounding the observer to which they could apply. Thus a sound source which is, for instance, lying ahead at 15 degrees off the starboard bow produces the same intensity, frequency, time and phase differences as a sound source which has a bearing of 180°−15° = 165°. Here we have to contend with similar conditions as those which occur with radio direction finders. Once these have been aligned to a null, the transmitter can lie in either of two directions differing by 180 degrees. Our auditory system solves this problem, as Figure 16 shows, by making tiny head movements while locating the sound. The false source would have to move by up to double the angle of the head movement in order to produce the same stimuli as the true source, which remains in a constant position in the right direction.

Head movements also enable us to locate sound sources which are not directly in front or behind – for instance 45 degrees to the side – with greater ease and certainty. The searching motion of the head in attempting to locate a fog horn, for instance, will thus always align the head at an angle to the sound transmitter.

In practice a correct and sure location of sound sources is difficult because there are conditions which distort the speed and direction of

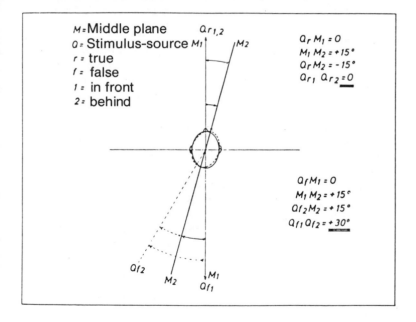

Figure 16. By moving our head (M_1–M_2) we can tell whether a sound source (Q) is located behind or in front of us.

the spread of the sound waves. Here we have to consider the refraction of the sound in different temperatures and densities of air as well as the manifold distorting effects of the wind. Despite the degree of accuracy which can theoretically be achieved, therefore, the sailor should only rely upon his capacity for locating acoustically the direction and distance of foghorns, whistle buoys, signalling vessels etc. in fog, when seafaring considerations or technical aids (such as radar) leave him no other option. There are many well-known examples of vessels colliding with other vessels or running into shallows because the sound of a foghorn has been perceived to be coming from the wrong direction or has not been heard at all.

The following anecdote may serve to underline once more the problematic nature of locating the direction and distance of sound sources.

When underway in the western Baltic with the two-masted top schooner *Godeke Michels* we were suddenly engulfed in the entrance to the Little Belt by thick fog. As we were on a crossing course, the watch leader could not be sure of our exact position. Several members of the crew located sound signals which seemed to be coming from a whistle buoy. In any event, we could not agree at first on its direction. It had to be some distance away as it was irregular and not very loud. After a short time the crew claimed to have located at least two whistle buoys, one to port and one to starboard. A glance at the chart convinced me of something I had suspected all along: there was no whistle buoy within miles that could still have been heard. After the crew had meanwhile agreed on 3 whistle buoys I searched the deck and found an empty beer bottle in front of the deckhouse – the sounds had been produced by the wind blowing across its neck. The gently muffled whistling on board had been interpreted as the distant whistling of a buoy. As the direction could not be clearly established, or rather didn't accord with the distance, various interpretations as to the source of the noise arose according to the position of each crewmember. Perhaps it would be wise to go back to buying cans for the next cruise.

Which is the right horizon? – contrast, irradiation, equalisation

To see is to see contrasts. In fog where there are no contrasts we hardly see anything, even though there are a great many sufficiently strong light stimuli striking the retina. The problem lies in the fact that these light stimuli are all of equal intensity; this gives rise to what is known in psychology as a 'homogeneous Ganzfeld'. In such circumstances one sees neither objects nor spatial depth, it is not even possible to judge the distance of something like a wall. This is why fog has such a disorientating effect. However in such a context even the finest light contrasts can be recognised as concrete objects. It is amazing the nuances the eye is able to discern: how we are able, for instance, to recognise the rigging of a topsail schooner in fog from what appears to be little more than a few irregular shadows. The best camera in the world could not perform as well. The eye manages it through two mechanisms:

(1) the sharp edge contrast (see Fig. 17) by which fields of almost equal brightness appear darker at their edges so that they stand out from each other relatively clearly; and

(2) subjective contours – in order to reproduce the environment and the objects contained therein realistically, our perceptual system possesses a so-called 'closure tendency' which, by adding subjective contours to objects which have been incompletely reproduced by the visual system, brings about their completion (see Fig. 18).

In clear visibility, on land and at sea, objects are generally well distinguished from each other. Finer contrasts which in fog would still have rendered a complete percept are suppressed in conditions of high visibility by the presence of sharp contrasts. Surfaces whose brightness is continually changing are seen in the presence of sufficiently stronger contrasts to be of uniform brightness (Equalisation). Contrast related phenomena are especially important to the seaman when observing the horizon in order to read the height of stars. A sufficiently well defined horizon is a prerequisite for an accurate measurement in which, as we all know, even the smallest errors can cause very great and dangerous misjudgements of position. Two heights measured incorrectly by only 2′ can lead to being out of position by 4 nautical miles in any direction. Every celestial navigator is aware that a horizon distorted by high humidity does not lend itself to accurate measurement of the altitude of stars: on the other hand, a horizon that is clearly defined, but which on account of subjective or objective conditions is illusory, can prove to be more dangerous.

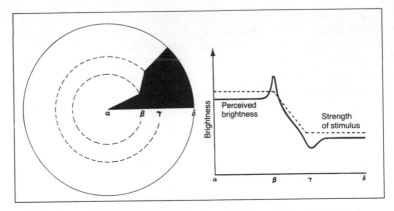

Figure 17. When the disk on the left is spinning rapidly, lines of contrast appear at the edges of the different areas of brightness at points β and γ as represented in the diagram on the right.

Figure 18. Subjective contours: the outline of the upright triangle is clearly perceptible even though only small sections are actually represented.

For instance, when the sun is low in the sky, the horizon below appears to lie higher. In contrast, the moon horizon at night lies below the real horizon. What causes these illusions?

Figure 19 shows how the sun, when it is low in the sky, creates a strong reflection on the water. This contrasts brightly with the somewhat darker background of the sky. The stretches of water to

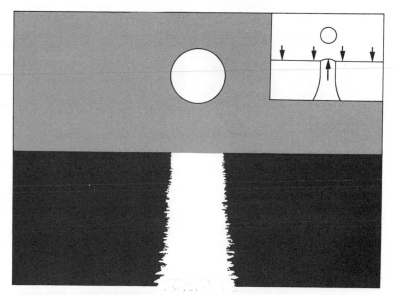

Figure 19. The horizon below the sun seems to curve upwards (see text).

either side of the sun's reflected path stand out darkly against the sky in comparison. At the light-dark borders an area of haziness arises on account of, amongst other things, tiny, imperceptible, rapid movements of the eye. The size of this indistinct area is dependent on the degree of contrast: the stronger the contrast, the larger the area. It is generally added to the lighter field. This effect is called irradiation (see Fig. 20) and gives rise to a (subjective) displacement of the horizon resulting in a perceived upcurve immediately under the sun. The resultant errors in angles of height can be avoided if one reduces the contrast at the horizon by fitting a filter in front of the horizon glass on the sextant. On the index mirror the overstrong contrast due to the sun has already been reduced by an appropriate filter.

The Moon Horizon at night poses a slightly different problem. On a clear night the moon also reflects its path on the surface of the water and we believe we can clearly see the horizon at the end of the reflection. Figure 21, however, shows (with the actual relations strongly exaggerated) that the contrast rich horizon created by the moonlight lies far in front of the actual, poorly contrasted horizon.

Figure 20.   Irradiation: both inner squares are the same size yet the white one seems larger.

The latter, owing to the strong contrasts of the Moon Horizon, remains invisible to us – to our eyes it is part of the surrounding darkness. The real sextant height of the moon is therefore always less than the one measured from the moon horizon. In this situation additional optical information is of no use either. In lower and medium latitudes, at least, we have to dispense with sextant readings of the moon at night. In high latitudes the fact that the sun sinks only a little below the horizon may produce a permanent twilight and thereby facilitate measurement of the height of stars all through the night.

The colourful world of sailing – a little on colour perception

The environment of the sailor is, for the most part, relatively uniform in terms of colour. Blue, grey and green colour tones predominate albeit in many nuances and shades. Colours have an impressionistic rather than an expressionistic character. Those which are rich in contrast and highly saturated are rare, and as a rule are due to other vessels (a spinnaker perhaps) or land objects.

Nevertheless, anyone who wishes to take the helm responsibly or who is involved in the command of a ship must have a good capacity for colour differentiation. On average 10 per cent of all men will have difficulties in obtaining this certificate as this is the frequency with which congenital colour blindness involving the red-green spectrum is distributed through the population. Women, among whom defective colour vision is considerably less common, have a real chance here to prove their superiority!

The psychological and physiological mechanisms of colour perception have been intensively researched for over 150 years and yet

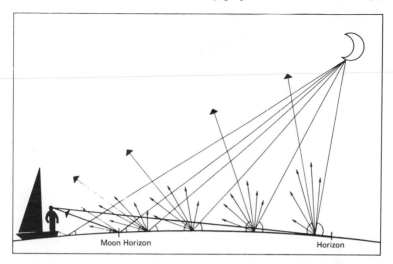

Figure 21. The Moon Horizon: most of the moonlight is reflected off the water surface into space in accordance with the optical laws (angle of incidence = angle of refraction). This is why in moonlight we see the horizon to be lower and nearer than it really is.

even today we still cannot claim to comprehend them fully. It has been established, however, that with regard to the physio-chemical processes in the retina there is a three colour system, so that from the wavelengths for red, blue and green, all other colours can be additively mixed (colour television is based on this phenomenon). On a psychological level it is easier to think in terms of two complementary colour systems – a red-green system and a yellow-blue system – according to which colour adaptation and colour vision defects may be explained.

In the uniformly coloured surroundings of the sea the smallest contrast-rich points of colour can be recognised at long range long before the other attributes of an object – in the case of buoys, long before their form, let alone their topmarks are recognizable. Red buoys are generally much easier to recognise from a distance than green buoys. Recognition of green buoys has been made much easier in many waters by the introduction of fluorescent paint. Green buoys which are non-fluorescent, at a distance, look black.

They also tend to stand out less well against the blue-green background.

A well-known illusion, frequently reported by seafarers, occurs when buoys with bright green lights at long range, at night, initially appear yellowish in colour (and are therefore easily confusable with buoys with white lights), while buoys with white lights, in the distance, have a reddish glow on first sight. One can observe the same phenomenon with the setting sun, which assumes an increasingly reddish colour at the horizon. These changes in colour, however, do not have any psychological basis but are determined by the physical properties of the atmosphere which acts as a filter on light waves of different wavelengths.

Figure 22 represents the spectrum of visible light: short-wave light appears blue, long-wave red, and in-between lie the remaining colours of the rainbow. Since the air is never completely pure but interspersed with steam, particles of dust, bacteria (even air plankton), light waves travelling through the air are diffused. This scattering effect is essentially much stronger in the case of short-wave than with long-wave light. This also explains why the aforementioned changes of colour take place when light waves travel for greater distances through the air. Green light is composed of both blue and yellow light; the short-wave bluish light is more diffused by air plankton, leaving a predominantly yellowish light. White light consists of a mixture of light of all wavelengths. When the short-wave (blue-green) light is filtered out, the yellow and red light remains,

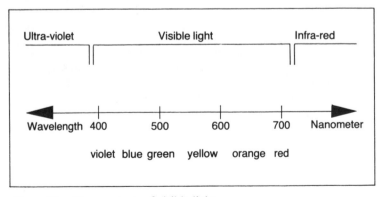

Figure 22.   The spectrum of visible light.

and so white light from a greater distance is more likely to assume a reddish tinge.

This only applies, however, to actual sources of lightwaves. The atmosphere itself and weaker sources of light are more likely to appear bluish in the distance.

Thus the colour of an object at sea, of a buoy for instance or another vessel, assists in the judgement of its distance. Red colours generally appear closer than blue colours. This may be accounted for by the fact already mentioned that distant and weak sources of light take on a slightly blue tinge; from this we learn to see red objects as being closer. It is, however, important to know that in twilight the effect is reversed: in this case blue objects appear closer than red objects because when the eyes are accustomed to the dark they are more sensitive to blue than to red light. Correspondingly red buoys look black in the increasing dusk.

What is moving, what isn't moving? – perceived motion is relative

The moving navigational light – auto-kinetic phenomena

You are standing on deck in the dead of night, visibility is average, it is just possible to make out the horizon. The crew are looking out for a navigational light of 1 flash every 10 seconds. Someone spots something and calls 'three points ahead on the port bow'. After a short while the skipper also sees a flash ahead on the port bow and begins to count off the signal, keeping his eyes steadily fixed – as if spellbound - on the point at which he has seen the flash: 9, 10, 11, 12, 13, 14, ... no flash appears. After a further 16 seconds he sees the flash again – two points ahead on the port bow. He counts again – 10 seconds later the flash comes – but at four points. There is no such thing as a navigational light which can change its position. Nor, according to the chart, is it possible for there to be two navigational lights in the area. The only remaining explanation is that here we are dealing with a subjective phenomenon.

If one watches a fixed point of light in a completely darkened room for some time it will soon begin to move: it may move in either a horizontal or vertical direction depending on the perception of the individual observer. Psychologists call this phenomenon the 'auto-kinetic illusion'. Imperceptible movements of the eyes, or even simply changes in the tension of the eye muscles when we exert ourselves to fix on a point, are responsible for this. The first case involves a real displacement of the point of light on the retina. In the second case, an isometric alteration in the tension of the eye muscle (without the eye moving) leads the organism to assume that a displacement of the point of light on the retina will occur. In both cases the brain interprets the data as a movement of the real point of light, since in the pitch-black surroundings there is nothing else that could represent itself as movement on the retina.

It is thus the lack of a frame of reference that is chiefly responsible for the illusory movement of the light. At sea at night we still have a horizontal frame of reference in the horizon, although this only rules out a navigational light jumping in a vertical direction. In the horizontal plane, because there are no other points of reference, an individual flash may resurface again and again at different points on the horizon. Inaccurate helming with, for instance, deviations from the course to the order of 10–20 degrees would naturally make things worse. Such slow yawing of the boat remains subliminal to the watchman due to the inertia of his organs of balance, and therefore goes completely unnoticed. The resultant change in the bearing of the sought-for navigational light must, therefore, be likewise interpreted as a change in its position. If the worst comes to the worst and this effect is coupled with the auto-kinetic illusion, considerable illusory transpositions of navigational lights can result.

The auto-kinetic illusion naturally also occurs with fixed position lights on shore. Thus, in certain circumstances (namely when there are no other points of reference), it is extremely difficult to tell the difference between a white light on the stern of a boat and a lighthouse: we will always see slight movements due to auto-kinesis (and possible helming errors). In view of this potential for confusion, it would be better if navigational lights did not use the fixed white signal which, fortunately, is seldom the case anyway. This problem will, however, be familiar to any sailor who, coming from the lightship *Elbe 1*, has been looking out for the white light of the Alte Weser.

The auto-kinetic illusion is also very prone to 'suggestion'. If several crewmembers are in dispute over the direction of movement of a solitary stern light or perhaps of a fixed navigational light (the perception of which is subjective and therefore possibly variable as we have seen), the skipper need only insist that the light is moving astern and within a short time (provided his authority is unchallenged) the rest of the crew will be in agreement with him. This is an example of how socially determined our perception is.

Jumping lights – stroboscopic movement

A special kind of movement effect occurs when several flashing or occulting buoys appear from a certain perspective to be more or less in a line. An apparent jumping of light from buoy to buoy may then be observed according to the coordination of the on/off rhythm. On the roads this kind of stroboscopic effect is sought purposefully in order, for instance, to signal the beginning of roadworks. However, at sea such manifestations of light can be confusing since they are not scheduled in the International Regulations for Preventing Collisions at Sea.

For the eyes there is always a definite impression of movement when one light appears immediately after another has gone out somewhere else. The impression of movement (which incidentally cannot be differentiated from the perception of a rapid, real movement) is not lessened if the light changes colour (from red to green for instance) on the way.

The wandering moon – induced movement

As we have seen with the auto-kinetic illusion, for a clear perception of movement, at least two objects have to be seen in relation to each other. If the distance between the two objects changes, one of them at least must be moving – provided it is not the observer himself. Which of the two objects it is is not immediately discernible. Here the same rules apply to our perception as in the theory of relativity in physics. Whether one says the sailor is moving towards the coast or the coast is moving towards the sailor, is, at first, totally immaterial. That this should only be so for the theoretical physicist and not, fortunately, in practice for the seaman, lies in the fact that over millions of years of adaptation to the different stimuli on earth our perception mechanisms have taken probability into account. If a small object is displaced against a larger object or surrounding frame, the small or enclosed object is the one that is moving. One may count on this rule leading to an accurate portrayal of reality in over 99% of all cases. Generally speaking, animals, people, cars, boats etc. move in front of a background; the background does not move past immobile objects or organisms. We can test the validity of this by following the moving object or organism with our eyes; the background moves across the retina at more or less the same speed.

When, however, the real relations are reversed for once, because our perceptual system obeys the above rule 100%, we become victims of an illusion. Anyone who has ever watched the moon at night in broken cloud will be familiar with this illusion: the moon seems to drift by behind the stationary fields of cloud. It does this against our better judgement since, compared to the clouds, it is (to all intents and purposes) fixed. (We can ignore the much slower independent movement of the moon in this connection). Psychologists describe this effect as 'induced movement' since in this illusion the movement does not exist objectively but is rather induced by the associated field.

The induced movement of stationary objects by the associated field is a fairly common occurrence at sea. A large freighter travelling slowly past a buoy not too far in the distance creates the impression that the buoy is drifting away in the opposite direction. Figure 23 gives another example of this. Objectively the two outer boats are moving to the right. It appears instead, however, that the boat at anchor between them is moving to the left.

Relative movements at sea are of course not always so plain as they are in this case, and events are not always so easily recognised as

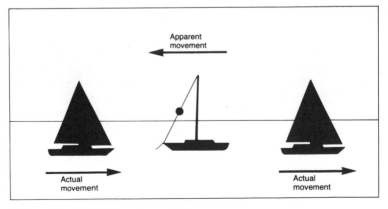

Figure 23.   Which boat is moving?

illusions. At night in particular, in busy shipping lanes or traffic seperation zones, it is often difficult to tell straight away which light is moving in which direction and which light is not making headway at all. It becomes especially difficult when there are several craft travelling at angles to us at varying distances. When two vessels are travelling through the water at the same speed the angular velocity of

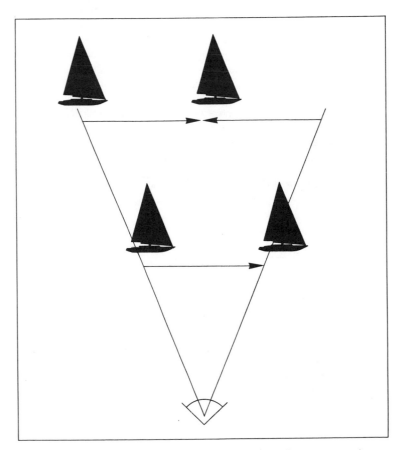

Figure 24. Movement is relative: the more distant sailor appears to be moving more slowly than the nearer one although objectively he covers the same distance.

the craft furthest from us is less than that of the boat nearer us. Despite clear identification of the side lights we still often get the impression that the more distant boat is moving in the opposite direction to that of the nearer boat (see Fig 24). In such cases special care needs to be taken when appraising the overall situation and the skipper would do well to take note of the movement illusions described here.

The judgement of relative movement becomes even more complicated when we sail in unfamiliar waters (in regions, for example, where the tidal currents are not known to us). For instance, if we are heading towards the coast and an object located between ourselves and the coast seems to be moving with respect to the latter, it can just as easily be the case that we ourselves are being displaced in the opposite direction by the wind or current.

Newcomers to radar observation often have special difficulties in reading the screen. Here one's own craft is usually represented as the stationary centre point. The movements of other vessels and objects are therefore always relative to our own craft. A vessel travelling towards us, for instance, can only be distinguished from one we are in the process of overtaking ourselves by the different speeds of approach on the radar screen. Our own speed on the screen is, so to speak, annulled, and it requires quite a bit of imagination and experience to interpret movements on the screen correctly.

Attention and strain in prolonged observation – lookout and radar

The psychological problems of radar observation and interpretation are among the best researched areas of psychology at sea. Indeed a certain field of research in applied psychology – research into vigilance (examination of the attention span) took as its starting point the problems of radar observation during the Second World War. Already at that time it had been noticed that more than half of all sightings of alien craft were made within the first half hour of radar watches lasting two hours or more (see Fig 25). Since it is safe to assume that the average number of craft encountered is independent of the length of time the observer has been on watch, it must also be assumed that after half an hour the attention drops off considerably. It is true that radar sets are still not very common on yachts and that,

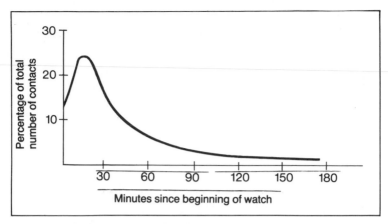

Figure 25. The influence of watch duration on the percentage of signals that are detected on the radar screen.

on the boats that do have them, there would not normally be regular watches taking place round the clock. However, if a yacht is equipped with radar and the skipper is relying on radar navigation in conditions of bad visibility or fog, he should arrange watch relief every 30 minutes. After all, what good is technically lavish and costly equipment if only a small percentage of all potential collisions are identified in time because of the limitations of the human capacity for perception and concentration?

Another project investigated the length of time it takes for a collision course to be recognized. The findings show that during the first half an hour of a watch a collision course is recognized as such after 20 to 25% of its 'running time' on the radar screen. By running time we mean the period of time between the appearance of a pip on the edge of the screen and its arrival at the centre (or collision point). After an hour on watch the collision course is only recognized after 60% of its running time and after 2 to 3 hours, only once the approaching pip has been visible for 75% of the time available for reaction. In isolated cases the collision course is only noticed once there has (theoretically) already been an accident. These findings not only show that concentration cannot be sustained for longer than half an hour but, over and above this, they also show that the familiar problems in interpreting the screen when navigating by radar may be

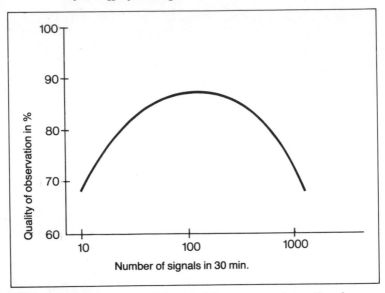

Figure 26.   The influence of the signal frequency on the quality of observation.

considerably increased in proportion to the length of time spent on watch.

Another important factor in radar observation is the number of signals which appear within a given time. If only 10 signals occur in half an hour the quality of observation is 70%, which means that only 70% of the signals are seen. The low probability of a potential collision course appearing, then, causes the level of concentration to fall. If 100 signals occur in 30 minutes the quality of observation rises to almost 90%. With an even greater number of signals, it drops considerably again. Thus, when there are few signals the quality of observation is low because the attentive capabilities of the brain are under-used, while when there are a great many signals it is low because these capabilities are being overtaxed (see Fig 26). In busy shipping channels one has to make allowances for 30% or more of the signals on the radar scope not being noticed. This percentage may be equally as high when there is seldom anything visible on the screen. Our powers of concentration function best with a medium signal density.

Another finding from the research into radar observation, which is also of interest to the yachtsman, is the fact that we tend to over-estimate the speed of craft on the screen. The lower the objective speed of the vessel the greater the over-estimation. The most serious mistakes are made when we are trying to locate stationary objects. An important consideration in this connection is that the information afforded by the radar on board a boat is relative in the sense that the entire field of surveillance moves across the screen at the speed of one's own craft. One might assume that over-estimation of the speed of vessels on a collision course is a permissible error since in reality the margin of safety is always going to be greater. This however is not the case as Figure 27 demonstrates. According to its assumed (over-

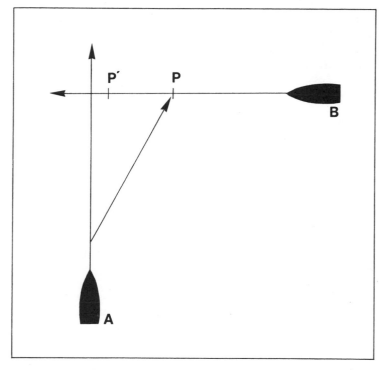

Figure 27. Collision danger through over-estimation of speed on the radar screen; see text.

estimated) speed, B would, at the point where A (our craft) crosses its course, have reached position P'. In view of this we change course to pass astern of him. According to his actual, lower speed, however, B has only just arrived at position P, making a collision inevitable.

Many of the more thoroughly researched problems concerning the attention span during radar observation also apply to the ordinary look-out on vessels which do not have radar. Similar limitations to one's capacity for observation also exist here, especially as the look-out has a much greater physical area to scan and monitor than a radar screen. Here there is the additional problem of chronologically classifying and generally assessing several separate observations which are made consecutively. The radar observer is able to command a more or less complete view of his area of supervision at any one time. The look-out on the other hand has only a very limited angle of vision in which clear sightings are possible and so he must piece together many individual situations, which are viewed one after the other, into a unified picture of the general position. Because this is very demanding mentally a look-out can, in busy areas and in bad visibility, become overtaxed relatively quickly.

Relative movements on the goggle-box – problems of radar interpretation

As we have already seen on page 42, the movements of vessels at sea are in the first instance 'relative' movements. This becomes a particularly disturbing and confusing problem in radar observation. From our experience of driving on land we are used to having a stable environment in which it is easy to classify our own movements and those of other road users. This is not the case at sea: here the surroundings are uniform and variable. The movement of the waves does not correspond in any constant sense to a particular direction of flow but is simply made up of the circular motion of waves of energy. The movement of water over ground, which we call tidal flow, bears no direct relation to the apparent directional course of the waves as produced by the wind. Without the use of landmarks such as buoys it is difficult to determine the tidal flow. Indeed it is only possible if we calculate the difference between the position of the boat as determined by dead reckoning and its true position (i.e. as it is influenced by the wind and current). Thus we sometimes find ourselves sailing relatively hard to windward and apparently making good headway when we are actually moving backwards owing to a strong current. It is well known that the speed over ground cannot be read from the log on yachts or small vessels – this is only possible with the help of other electronic aids to navigation. At sea the movement of other craft is always seen in relation to our own movement. In this respect radar observation is not essentially different to observation with the naked eye. Why then should assessment of the course and speed of potential collision partners on the radar screen be so much more difficult?

Firstly, with the naked eye we perceive our own craft and thereby our point of reference to be in motion. Because of this the perceptible speed through the water is quite sufficient for judging the course and speed of other craft since any possible unknown tidal currents will influence our ground speed in the same way as that of the others. On the radar screen, however, our own vessel is represented as the stable point in the centre which, owing to a lack of other information such as bow waves, wake and so on, suggests that the boat is unmoving while the relative movements of other boats and objects appear as absolute movements. This is why a contact moving towards us on the radar screen seems to swing out to port if our own craft makes a change in course to port. Our course alteration is not represented on the screen. With the naked eye we may find that this contact was no more than a fixed buoy. In principle one can say that on the radar our own movement, in terms of direction and speed, is vectorially added to the movement of the contact.

Correct evaluation of the absolute movement of alien vessels is, even after years of experience, so difficult that collisions occur time after time with the 'help' of the radar. How they come about is demonstrated in almost every book and course on the subject.

A classic example of this type of situation was the collision between the two luxury liners the *Andrea Doria* and the *Stockholm* on 25 July 1956. The whole episode is simplified and schematically represented in Figure 28. In thick fog the *Andrea Doria* passes south of the Nantucket lighthouse on a westerly course of 268 degrees. On the radar unit a small pip appears on the starboard bow at a distance of about 12nm. The captain of the *Andrea Doria* assumes that it is a trawler heading for Nantucket Island, due north of him. He therefore sees no reason to change course in order to pass the oncoming vessel in accordance with the international regulations (port to port),

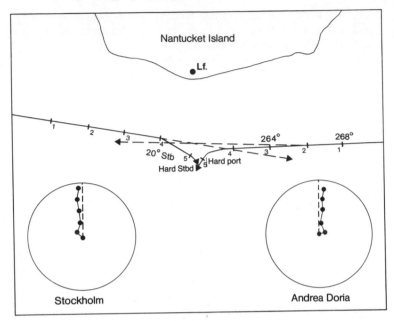

Figure 28.   Collision with radar support (see text).

particularly as he would prefer to avoid the northerly shallows in front of Nantucket Island. But, as the oncomer approaches, it becomes clear from the radar that she may get dangerously close to the *Andrea Doria*. In view of this the captain decides to alter course by 4 degrees to port(!). The *Stockholm* has also seen the oncoming ship on the port side. When they have closed to within 3 ½ nm he decides to alter course by 20 degrees to starboard in order to pass the oncomer, by the book, red to red. In the meantime the fog has broken up and on board the *Andrea Doria* the *Stockholm* is seen close-to showing a red as opposed to the expected green starboard light. The captain issues a command of hard-a-port while at the same time on board the *Stockholm*, which is at last making a positive attempt to get out of the way of the *Andrea Doria*, hard-a-starboard is ordered. Only now has the collision become completely unavoidable and the reinforced prow of the *Stockholm* rams into the *Andrea Doria* at bridge level.

When ships approach each other at an acute angle in this way the result has frequently been 'radar supported' collisions, and this has, at times, brought radar technology into disrepute. We are going to look essentially at the psychological aspects of this dangerous and fairly typical situation.

First of all, we should again become clear in our minds that there is an important difference between the direct perception of an encounter with another vessel and the representation of this encounter on the radar screen: with the naked eye we can not only determine the bearing of the other vessel but we can also roughly assess its course. Even in the dark, navigation lights permit us to tell exactly in which direction another vessel is travelling. On the radar screen, however, we only see a pip at a certain bearing and the relative movement of the contact is at best indicated by a small tail. Only after a certain amount of time has elapsed are we able, by plotting its progress, to judge more accurately its motion in relation to our own. By negative fixing of the ground covered between two radar observations, taking our own speed and heading into account, we can also determine the course of a contact. Information as to which side of another vessel is facing us is almost completely lacking and we can only roughly and, in view of the discussion below of potential errors, inaccurately determine whether its course will cut across our own or not. It is even more difficult to establish whether an oncoming vessel cutting across our course at an acute angle will, if each vessel maintains its heading, pass ahead or astern (a high degree of inaccuracy is inevitable in judging the point of intersection in such situations).

The example shows furthermore that when movement is relative in this way small changes in course are not discernible on the radar screen. If two craft are moving towards each other with a combined speed of 40 knots, even a 20 degree course change by the oncoming craft produces such a fine alteration in its relative course that the change remains subliminal and cannot be discerned. With vessels travelling at high speed course changes are only clearly noticeable when they exceed 60 degrees; even with slow moving craft, however, 90 degree course changes should be introduced in the interests of safety.

The reason we find it so fiendishly difficult to interpret acute-angled movements on the radar screen is, however, that we fall prey to a perceptual illusion which has now been more thoroughly researched and which will be discussed below. This perceptual illusion is a consequence of the fact that our perceptual system orders the environment into four spatial directions. If we drop something it falls vertically downwards, trees and plants grow (more or less) vertically upwards. The horizon or, as we say at sea, the visual or apparent horizon, is aligned at right angles to the direction of gravity.

Correspondingly our eyes discern vertical and horizontal lines particularly successfully and precisely. Everything that lies between is much less distinct and is less accurately perceived. The highest areas of inaccuracy are found directly adjoining those of greatest accuracy, namely, directly next to the vertical and the horizontal. An angle that only deviates a little from 90 degrees – measuring 89 degrees for instance or 91 degrees – is usually perceived as a right angle. This tendency to distort perceptions towards the 'preferred' vertical and horizontal vectors is called *Prägnanz*. Prägnanz means on the one hand that these preferred directions, forms etc. are more salient and perceived more quickly while, on the other hand, it also means that slight deviations from these 'absolute' vectors or forms are perceptually distorted (or 'rectified') to produce the more concise, regular and simple configuration.

Thus in looking at the different spatial directions on a compass card for instance, we can construct a so-called 'Prägnanz function' so that 0, 90, 180, and 270 degrees, are highly marked while directly next to these preferred points are areas of very low Prägnanz. Perceptions in the unfavoured areas will tend to be distorted towards the preferred points, while the areas around NE, SE, SW and NW are neither high nor low in Prägnanz and are relatively indistinct in the terms of this descriptive framework.

The Gestalt psychologists' theory of Prägnanz accords with the empirical findings of radar research. Figure 29 shows the results of an experiment in which a significantly higher percentage of collision courses were identified correctly at the four main points of the compass than courses at points in-between. Potential collision courses which appeared directly beside the main points were the ones most poorly perceived. We are thus equally able to identify a potential collision partner coming directly towards us as one whose relative course is at right angles to our own on the radar screen. In the intermediate areas of the quadrants in which, in practice, most approaching vessels may appear, judgements on a potential collision are considerably less accurate. Over and above this it was proved in the same experiment that approaches at an acute angle to the vertical

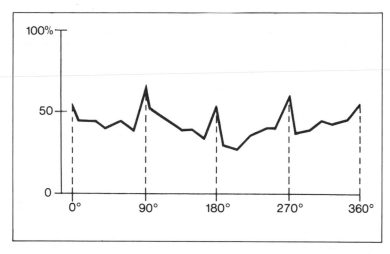

Figure 29.   Correct perception of a collision course at different bearings on the radar screen (in %).

(or almost at right angles and hence near the horizontal) were distorted perceptually. This can very easily lead to false judgements on the question of whether the course of an identified contact ahead will cross our own or not and if so, whether it will pass ahead or astern of us.

The danger of the acute angled encounter and its possible misinterpretation on the radar screen is thus based in the first instance on a perceptual psychological illusion. Recognition of this fact should prompt us to follow the International Regulations for Preventing Collisions at Sea to the letter in such situations – namely by responding in good time with a decisive change in course to starboard.

We have seen that considerable problems arise both in radar observation and in the interpretation of relative movements on the radar screen. Some assistance is indeed provided by modern technology, but this is essentially only of benefit to ocean-going shipping; readings from a north stabilised radar in conjunction with a gyrocompass mean that the course changes of one's own craft become clearly perceptible; and with true-motion radar, on which one's own craft moves across the radar screen as well as the other vessels, relative motion no longer exists and the absolute movements of all vessels may be read directly. The portrayal of absolute movement in true-motion radar does, however, have one disadvantage which was brought to light in an empirical investigation – collision courses are even more difficult to recognise than when the screen is showing the relative movements. This makes sense if we recall that with the latter it is possible to determine roughly whether a contact will meet the centre point, and hence our own craft, by extending its tail. With the absolute representation of the movement of vessels, however, these extensions will always intersect (except in the case of parallel courses) and so more complicated calculations are required in order to identify a collision course.

Nevertheless yachtsmen should continue to work with the course stabilised radar if they possess such a navigational aid. It should, however, have become clear that observation and interpretation of the radar, when other information is lacking due to bad visibility, demand increased effort and concentration and do not, therefore, constitute an easy option.

How to identify a navigational light without a stopwatch – the perception and estimation of time

Many yachtsmen may perhaps still recall how their sailing instructor tried to drum into them that when attempting to identify the recurring signal of a navigational light they should not rely on their own judgement of time but on a stopwatch alone. A flashing 6s could, without precise timekeeping, be just as easily taken for a Fl. 8s as for a Fl. 4s. Exact identification of navigational lights starts to become difficult with longer dark pauses such as Fl. 20s (1 flash every 20 seconds). Moreover, judgement of time is – and there is certainly psychological truth in this – subject to the suggestiveness of what is desired. What skipper would not like, at long last, to make out ahead of him the characteristic (as described on the chart) of a buoy he has been in search of for hours? In such contexts it is possible to make one's counting fit any interval one likes.

And yet in reality there is another side to the story: at night the stopwatch is rarely to hand and when it is, we cannot see it because there is not enough light. Furthermore, even if we were to use a torch this would reduce our eyes' adaption to the dark, so that, in order to repeat the measurement, we would need more time to reaccustom ourselves to the gloom in order to relocate the navigation light – which is probably weak as it has just been sighted. In short, there is still something to be said for simply counting out the signals. And, this being the case, it is a good idea to test one's capacity for temporal perception before the cruise and perhaps even try to improve it through practice. But first, a little theory.

There is a distinction to be drawn between the 'perception' and the 'estimation' of time. With the perception of time we are speaking of intervals of time of up to approximately 2 secs. This corresponds to the time we experience as the present moment. Longer intervals have to be consciously estimated. In contrast to the other sensory abilities, there is no one definite (anatomically locatable) sensory organ for either temporal perception or estimation. It is accepted that these depend on the biological rhythms which, as far as the slow rhythms are concerned, are in turn dependent on the planetary movements as they appear to us on Earth. The shorter divisions of time (hours, minutes, seconds) are arbitrary gradations of the day. The biological rhythms of higher frequency (breathing: approx. 15/min; pulse: approx. 70/min; alpha-rythm of the neural activity in the brain: 8-13/s) are independent of these time divisions. The valuation of years, months and days therefore comes very easily to us; it is only for divisions of time within the day that we need the aid of clocks. Nevertheless our capacity to judge hours, minutes and even seconds, is very good. We know from observing the behaviour of animals that, with regard to feeding times, they can be trained to the minute. Similarly people who have firmly resolved to wake up at a particular time frequently (although unfortunately not always) do so before the alarm goes off.

In assessing the accuracy of estimates of the passage of time, one should bear two simple rules in mind. Firstly, that such estimates are dependent on how active a person is; the greater the degree of activity within a given interval of time, the shorter it seems to be. Secondly, our experience of time is dependent on how much information we absorb through the senses: the more uniform (boring) the environment, the slower the time seems to pass.

In judging time intervals of up to 30 secs, these being the most important ones for the sailor, one should generally subdivide the time into (estimated) seconds by counting silently in two digit numbers (21, 22, 23 ...). This is a very sensible method since perceptual accuracy is at its greatest in judging intervals in the region of one second. The temporal perception of people who have no practice in this deviates on average by 8% from the actual time, while estimated time intervals between 5 and 30 secs are out by 16% on average – there is, in other words, double the degree of inaccuracy

The estimation of time intervals of up to 30 secs can be practised to good effect using a stopwatch as a control. By checking against the constant feedback from the watch it is possible to standardise one's judgement so that errors of less than 10 per cent arise in estimating intervals of the above duration. This is a tolerable degree of error since it would mean at the very worst that a navigational light which flashes every 10 seconds might be confused with one whose period is 11 seconds. It goes without saying that even greater accuracy in judging time intervals is possible through practice. This newly acquired ability to estimate an interval of one second can then be employed in gauging the length of sound signals as they are laid down in the International Regulations for Preventing Collisions at Sea. According to these regulations a longer tone should have a duration of 4 to 6 secs. I have, however, seldom come across a yachtsman who could keep his finger on the button of the foghorn for as long as this when sounding the attention signal.

2 *The psychological factors in seasickness*

Anyone can become seasick

Every yachtsman will have had to deal with the problems of seasickness before: whether he himself has had to bend surreptitiously over the rail or whether he has had to lend other members of the crew support and encouragement during an attack. If someone is affected by seasickness it does not mean that he or she is a hopeless landlubber. On the contrary it is a standard physical process which can only operate if one's organs of balance are 'healthy'. People (and animals) whose balance organs have been damaged or surgically removed do not get seasick. With the aforementioned exceptions, it is accepted today that at some point in life everyone is susceptible to seasickness to a certain degree in the event of the appropriate movement stimuli. This makes good 'biological' sense if we consider the fact that in evolutionary history it proved worthwhile for certain species, human beings among them, to avoid those conditions under which seasickness occurred – the sea in other words; a particularly unpredictable and dangerous environment. Over thousands of years, this gave these species an advantage in terms of natural selection. It is true that most people do get used to the constant motion stimuli when they are at sea for a long time and that their susceptibility to seasickness diminishes considerably, but the process of accustomisation varies from person to person, so that many an old seaman may still have to pay the price each time he is out in a storm – something which need not however interfere with his ability to command a ship. Look at Lord Nelson, who suffered regularly from seasickness and yet still managed to accomplish strategic feats at sea of the highest order. The occurrence of seasickness is by no means restricted to the environmental conditions of the sea, however. With the appropriate motion stimuli it can also arise in a car, on a train or aeroplane and, latterly, in space travel as well. As the triggering conditions and the symptoms are similar in each case it is generally referred to as 'motion sickness' (the medical term is 'kinetose').

Can seasickness be avoided without medicine?

Among those who sail for recreation there are two schools of thought for dealing with seasickness: one swears by medicinal aid and the other by self-reliance. This chapter will be concentrating on the second group. What follows, then, will not be a medical discourse in which the pros and cons of the various medicines for motion sickness are analysed, although there are certain disadvantages to taking medicine which should not be forgotten.

In the first place, medicines only work if they are taken according to directions, which, generally speaking, means 3 hours before the occurrence of the motion stimuli. In turn, this can mean 3 hours before going on board or 3 hours before the event of strong wind (less for those members of the crew particularly prone to seasickness). In practice these directions are rarely followed correctly. More often than not the tablets are taken at the first signs of illness, by which time the seasickness has already taken hold and it is too late for the medicine's prophylactic properties to take effect. Taking drugs has other disadvantages as well:

- Even if the medicines have been taken properly they often cause drowsiness, so that the afflicted member of crew may indeed be free to enjoy the cruise without feeling unwell or actually being sick, but as a result of the medication he can only do so asleep in his bunk.
- Most medicines overstrain the circulation.
- All medicines have potential, unwelcome side-effects which are often made much worse by taking other medicines or alcohol at the same time.

On the other hand there is a whole string of psychological conditions which can either bring on or prevent seasickness. Observance of the behavioural rules worked out in this chapter on the basis of current scientific findings can, to a certain extent, reduce the necessity for taking medicine and, for many yachtsmen, make it completely redundant. Certainly the psychological aspects of seasickness (just like the potential benefits afforded by medicine) should not be overestimated: the most significant factor in the occurrence of motion sickness is, and remains, motion. When one escapes from this motion and steps onto dry land again the complaint is for the most part 'cured' immediately.

The frequency, symptoms and course of seasickness

It is a realistic appraisal that, in the first two or three days of an Atlantic crossing in average sea and wind conditions, 25 to 30% of the passengers on board ship will become seasick. With sailors on small vessels this percentage can be even higher. In inflatable life rafts about 60% of the occupants will be affected by seasickness. In an American survey 90% of the 300 students questioned stated that they had experienced motion sickness at least once before. Certainly susceptibility can differ greatly from individual to individual; the threshold for the stimuli which trigger motion sickness is very variable. Reaction time also plays an important part: many people are affected as soon as they step on board a boat, others only after days of rough weather.

According to surveys that have been made, women become seasick more frequently and more quickly than men. Heightened susceptibility during menstruation possibly accounts for this statistical difference. Infants and older people are likewise supposed to be less susceptible than teenagers and younger adults. With infants this may have something to do with the fact that they spend most of their time on board lying down. Everybody is less likely to be affected when lying down. The decrease in susceptibility to motion sickness with age is possibly due to the fact that, with a longer life span, there has on average been more experience of the sea which has conditioned the adaptive mechanisms.

While this chapter may concentrate on the psychological aspects of seasickness, it should not be interpreted as suggesting that seasickness can be avoided altogether by psychological means. However, there is no doubt that the correct psychological approach can considerably raise the threshhold for the occurrence of the symptoms, and can initiate appropriate behaviour at the first signs of seasickness, thus preventing a further worsening of the conditions which lead to hours of vomiting.

All seamen will be familiar with the symptoms of motion sickness, which regularly occur in the following order: pallor, cold sweat, nausea and sickness. In addition to these there is a whole series of secondary factors which affect the behaviour and mood of those afflicted: weakness, dry mouth, headache, fatigue, need for fresh air, feeling of coldness, sensitivity to smell, apathy, the desire to be alone, indifference to companions, lack of motivation, lack of interest, spatial disorientation, anxiety and depression. Noticeable behavioural differences include: reduced spontaneity, carelessness, reduced muscle co-ordination and motor performance, poorer temporal judgement, and impaired mathematical ability. This list alone is indicative of the potentially problematic nature of entrusting someone suffering from seasickness, even though they have the best will in the world, to fulfill their duties on board, to navigate responsibly or to cope with dangerous work on deck which requires a high degree of physical control. It is, however, important that people suffering from seasickness are not unconditionally released from all duties on board but are assigned quite specific tasks.

The course seasickness takes with relatively inexperienced members of the crew always follows a similar pattern: from the moment of boarding the yacht one is conscious of increasing difficulties in adapting to the complex movements. The first signs of motion sickness, such as a slight headache and a dry mouth etc., appear and get progressively worse until after a lengthy period of feeling nauseous one is finally sick. This can recur for hours. After several days of uninterrupted sailing the victim regains control of his movements as he succeeds, through active compensatory movements, in maintaining his balance. Only now is he able to enjoy the cruise properly and apply himself to the tasks on board. It is unlikely that he will suffer a second attack on the same trip. When he goes ashore later however he will feel the after-effects of his adaption to the boat's movements, especially in narrow confined rooms or when lying down. The room seems to sway and it is difficult to keep one's balance. One might feel nauseous again or even be sick. This condition, which generally only lasts for a short time, is called 'land sickness'.

Which way up, which way down? - perception of the vertical

The sense of balance is as little able to distinguish between the force of gravity (gravitational pull) and additional accelerative forces (through movement) as any other physiological system. This is why on boats, in which we experience constant positive and negative acceleration in all spatial directions, there exists a force along the so-called apparent plumb line, which we perceive as 'down' and which

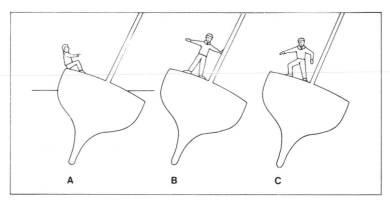

Figure 30. Perception of the vertical: (A) visually, (B) through the sense of balance and, (C) through the sense of position.

continually changes its direction. Here there arises a conflict between the apparent gravitational direction (changing with the movements of the boat) as registered by the sense of balance and the visually registered horizon which, in contrast, is stationary. This conflict of sensory information is a trigger for the autonomic symptoms connected with seasickness.

As a creature with an upright gait, perception of the vertical for the human being is of such fundamental importance that this information is monitored by three different sensory systems: the visual system, the sense of position and the sense of balance (see Fig 30).

This threefold cover is, as a rule, quite sufficient for standing upright and for locomotion on solid ground (whatever form this might take). At sea, however, where the deck of a boat is to a greater or lesser degree in constant acceleration and deceleration in three dimensions (pitch, roll, heading) and which in addition periodically moves along the axis of gravity (up and down movements), exceptionally high demands are made on these sensory systems in order to maintain an upright position. The additional forces of acceleration caused by the movements of the boat are, for us, indistinguishable from gravity since they add themselves to it vectorially (Fig 31).

We should at this point introduce a conceptual distinction: we call the direction of gravity, which is always at right angles to the horizon and which is perceived visually, the true vertical. Let us call the combined result of the gravitational pull and the additional forces on boats – the direction in which our physical balance is most easily maintained in an upright position – the perpendicular. This perpendicular is often also called the apparent plumb line.

Under normal (land) conditions the visual system responds most accurately to vertical lines (trees, walls of houses etc.). By accuracy we mean in this case that we not only perceive vertical lines more quickly but also recognize the slightest deviations from the vertical immediately (for instance crooked hanging picture frames!). The system also responds to horizontal lines with reasonable accuracy and

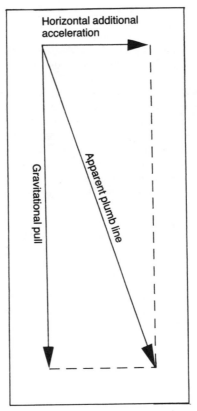

Figure 31.   Vectorial addition. The apparent plumb line as the result of gravitation and additional acceleration.

very much better than to all the angles between the two main vectors. While a deviation from the vertical or horizontal line of even one or two degrees is noticeable, most people cannot differentiate between lines or edges at angles of 40 degrees and 50 degrees (if they are not seen together). If the head, or even in fact the body itself, is at an angle this has little effect on the accuracy with which we perceive verticals and horizontals. This alone serves to indicate how closely the aforementioned sensory systems, which ensure our orientation in space, work together. For instance, when the head is at an angle of 30 degrees to the vertical an image appears on the retina at a corresponding angle. However, the relevant information from the sense of position (in the neck muscles and tendons) and the sense of balance (in the vestibular organ) is taken into account subconsciously.

At sea, information about the visual vertical is seldom available to us since masts, buoys, and so on almost always deviate from the vertical on account of the movement of the wind and water. In place of this we have in the horizon an almost ubiquitous horizontal line which is useful for our visual orientation in space.

The inclined position of a vessel from the vertical when it is listing or when it has gone aground is always greatly overestimated. If, for instance, the clinometer shows an angle of 30 degrees it is sure to have already been estimated by the crew to be over 45 degrees. Conversely we tend to underestimate the angle of heel when we are below deck and the saloon about us is following every listing movement. Here we are essentially reliant on information about the perpendicular from our organs of balance. This is particularly true if we are sitting down, in which case the sense of position plays only a very small part. If we look through the porthole, the horizon seems to move with the roll of the boat. This phenomenon is explained by the fact that besides the force of gravity which, at right angles to the horizon, is always directed towards the centre of the earth, there are additional forces of acceleration which affect our balance organs.

Figure 32 is an illustration of this: the continuous line represents the direction of gravity, the dotted line (perceived horizon) the additional accelerative force produced by the roll of the boat, and the (dotted) line at right angles to this indicates the result of these – the apparent plumbline which we perceive as the perpendicular. Since the organs of balance take this resultant force for the direction of gravity, the perceived horizon is classified in the perceptual space as

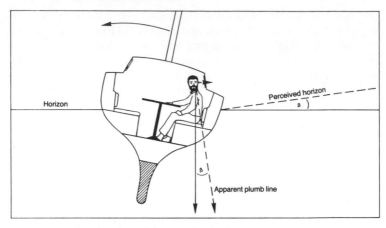

Figure 32.   The illusion of the swaying horizon.

being at right angles to the result of the relevant forces. It is true that the direction of gravity always remains constant whatever the movements of the boat, but the additional accelerations are continually changing direction and strength and hence also changing the combined result, so the horizon appears to be in constant motion. This effect occurs predominantly below deck because the horizon is only seen partially through the portholes or the saloon skylight and the visual impression is therefore comparatively poor. On deck however the horizon, which stretches all round the observer and which is visible from almost every head and body position, has a much stronger influence on our interpretation of the main parameters of the perceptual space.

On boats, particularly small yachts which are in constant rapid motion, information about the vertical line as it is received by the eyes is forever clashing with the information assimilated by our sense of position and sense of balance. When it comes to a conflict of sensations like this the visual system nearly always dominates. As mentioned earlier this perceptual conflict is one of the causes of seasickness.

More experience of the sea, however, means increasingly that the information about the perpendicular which becomes predominant is the result of gravitational pull and localised forces of acceleration as they affect the sense of balance. This means that one is better able to take an active part in the running of the boat since these are the forces which actually affect the body and against which compensatory movements have to be made to maintain the balance. An experienced yachtsman or seaman, therefore, seldom needs to support himself with his hands in order to keep his balance in the constant rolling and pitching of the boat, both hands being free instead for the work on deck.

Below deck one is initially thrown back and forth because the direction of gravity seems to be continually changing. With time, however, one learns to perceive the 'perpendicular' which arises from the movements of the boat and the direction of gravity. Thus the body maintains its balance when upright and learns to ignore the conflicting visual data afforded by the interior of the boat and the horizon outside the window.

Observation of gimballed objects (oil lamps, whisky bottles etc.) can be very helpful in developing spatial orientation on board, since they provide relatively constant information as to the best way to counteract the conflicting data.

What causes seasickness?

In the past the cause of seasickness was thought to lie in the workings of the stomach, just as in medicine generally whenever a symptom appeared there was assumed to be a physical cause. Today we know that seasickness arises through the operation of the balance organs in conjunction with the visual system and the brain. The triggering stimulus is motion.

Not all motion, however, makes us motion sick. Movements with a low frequency and greater amplitude are more likely to make us ill than movements with a high frequency and smaller amplitude (see Fig 33). It is reported, for instance, that people become motion sick riding camels but never through riding horses. Amplitudes of 2 to 5m with a frequency of 15/min, as commonly occur on boats, have the strongest effect. Susceptibility to motion sickness is increased when, in addition to the triggering motion stimuli, head movements are also made.

Experiments have shown that motion sickness is also triggered when the body and the ground below are stationary while the surrounding space turns periodically (see Fig 34). Anyone can

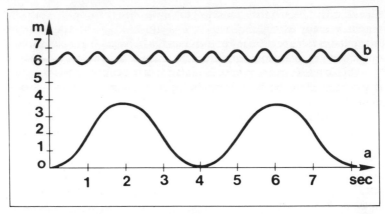

Figure 33. Forms of movement which trigger seasickness to a greater (a) or lesser (b) degree.

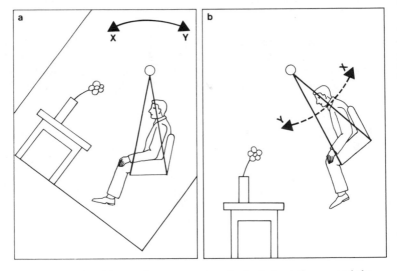

Figure 34. Seasickness also occurs when the body is stationary and the surrounding space is moved;
(a) the room moves periodically from x – y;
(b) however, it seems as if the subject is being swung from y – x.

observe this effect for themselves in the cinerama. The portrayal of sea crossings or air flights on screen can cause anyone who is standing in the room to have difficulty in keeping their balance and, in some cases, even to feel nauseous.

There are additional factors besides movement which can precipitate the syndrome. Obviously indigestible stomach contents, which under any other circumstances might cause one to be sick, increase the likelihood of seasickness. Many yachtsmen have also found that unpleasant fumes below deck or cooking smells from the galley can trigger the first symptoms of seasickness, which is why those who are at risk even in a swell seldom remain below deck of their own free will. The most important triggering factor, however, is the fear of seasickness.

The fear of illness is enough to make us ill

How often before have we heard friends who occasionally sail with us exclaim in protest, when told of the weekend plan to put into Heligoland, that they are always sick when they go there? Assurances from the skipper that the forecast is for light winds and that some swell is to be expected no matter where one is on the North Sea do not seem to help. There are people who, knowing they are going to Heligoland, become pallid and get a dry mouth as soon as they step on board. Indeed many even begin to feel seasick while still ashore at the mere sight of the boat. What is the reason for this?

This kind of anticipatory fear of seasickness is learnt or – in psychological terms – conditioned by one or more negative experiences in the past. The diagram in Figure 35 explains how this anticipatory fear, by which seasickness is triggered prematurely, arises.

On the left hand side of the diagram we have, to begin with, a simple conditioned reflex: heavy and continuous rolling and pitching of the boat produces reflexively (in other words without our exercising any conscious control over it) the symptoms of seasickness (pallor, sweating, nausea, sickness). Or, to put it another way: an unlearned (unconditioned) stimulus (UCS) produces an unlearned or inherent (unconditioned) reaction (UCR). Once a reflexive association of this kind has been activated on one or more occasions the conditions which always occur simultaneously with the UCS are

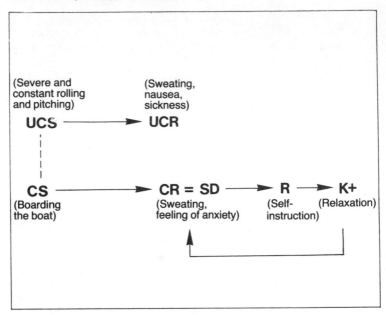

Figure 35.   How anticipatory fear arises and how it may be treated through relaxation (see text).

sufficient in themselves to call up a weakened seasickness response without the actual UCS (rolling and pitching) occurring: thus even the sight or boarding of a yacht can, as a learned (conditioned) stimulus (CS), give rise to a learned reaction (CR), such as anxiety and sweating.

The learned or conditioned reaction can, then, also occur in the absence of the original, typical motion stimuli which trigger seasickness. This learned reaction (CS – CR) can also be described as anticipatory fear reaction. On the basis of a conditioned reaction of this kind, once the boat puts to sea and the swell becomes noticeable, seasickness proper with its nausea and sickness will set in much more quickly. Anxious people, moreover, tend to sit quietly on board and submit passively to their fate. Motion sickness actually strikes people more quickly when they are sitting than when they are lying or standing (see page 70).

It is, however, not only the learned fear of seasickness that lowers the threshold for the appearance of the symptoms but also any kind of anxiety at sea or emotional strain in general. With many people, for example, nausea strikes whenever the boat is out of sight of the land.

If we look at the right hand side of the diagram (Fig 35) we are given a simple method for breaking down the learned or anticipatory fear. Psychologists call this therapy 'desensitization'.

One must learn to recognize the cause of anxiety (CR) in good time. It then becomes an easily discernible stimulus (SD). Next one should talk oneself through a relaxation exercise (R). A positive consequence (K) of this is a partial or complete relaxation of the muscles which counteracts the feeling of anxiety and with it the incipient seasickness. With time one manages to induce a relaxed state relatively quickly so that, in an emergency, the symptoms of anxiety can be overcome in a short time. Desensitization is one of the most widely utilized and successful psychological methods for reducing anxiety. There are of course other techniques as well, such as autogenous training (relaxation through self-hypnosis), that may be employed in physical relaxation.

What can we do about seasickness?

Members of the crew who are known to suffer anticipatory fear should be assigned a task by the skipper immediately they come on board. One of the features of such fear is that the victim's thoughts continually revolve around the seasickness ahead of them. Having something specific to do can deflect these thoughts. The task should be one that cannot be carried out sitting down but which requires varied activity designed specifically to prevent passive anticipation of the coming symptoms (for example, neatly coiling all the running gear lying around). When the body is in motion and both hands are employed, active compensatory movements have to be made against the boat's movements in order to keep one's balance. This makes adaption to the motion of the boat much easier. If, on the other hand, one is leaning against the rail or deckhouse, the body is simply rocked passively back and forth with the boat. This actually produces stronger motion stimuli in the vestibular organ and hinders active adaption.

The most suitable employment for a crew member who is prone to seasickness is helming. We know from our experience of motoring that passengers (on winding mountain roads, for instance) are frequently motion sick but never the driver himself. This is because the driver feels himself to be in control of the motion stimuli which he is actually triggering by his steering actions. Likewise on small sailing craft it is the helmsman who is least at risk from seasickness. Through having to hold a course he is similarly compelled to make active counter movements with the rudder against the yawing of the boat. The helmsman also tends to pay more attention to the swell than the rest of the crew and is thus prepared in advance for each movement the boat makes. In this case too, then, the feeling of being in control of the boat and its movements goes a long way towards preventing seasickness arising in the first place or towards quashing the initial symptoms.

As mentioned earlier, body position is also an important factor. In a prone position, seasickness occurs far less frequently or with less severe symptoms than when sitting. This is probably because, when lying down, the body does not lose its balance, and the head, in relation to the body, is relatively stable. Head movements in addition to the external motion stimuli serve to precipitate discomfort. The next most favourable position to lying down is to stand upright, legs slightly apart, without holding on to anything. One cannot avoid offsetting the movements of the boat in this position if one is to retain one's balance. Continuous reflexive compensatory movements are activated throughout the muscular system by the sense of balance and the sense of position, and this prevents a passive surrender.

A well known and relatively reliable preventative measure is to keep the eyes fixed on the horizon and the head always thus vertically aligned with it. This kind of head movement against the body, which permits a relatively constant (visual) perception of the direction of gravity, is the only one which does not intensify the symptoms of seasickness. For those susceptible to seasickness, however, this cannot avert the problem indefinitely since the conflict between what we see and our sense of balance continues to exist. All the same, placing crew members who are beginning to look pallid on look-out duty has occasionally proved worthwhile.

There are basically two methods for keeping one's balance on board without external support. One can respond to the oncoming waves which threaten to disrupt one's balance by making counter movements, or one can learn to anticipate the movements of the boat over the waves and adjust one's body position accordingly. In the first instance the gaze must be 'locked' onto the horizon or some other stable point of reference in order to restore the disrupted sense of balance. In the second instance the attention should be directed to windward in the direction of the oncoming waves since it is by anticipating these that we mean to adjust our balance. As the rhythm of the oncoming waves is relatively uniform, one soon acquires the knack of regulating one's balance in this way without it being necessary to estimate the effect of each individual wave in turn. This principle has become second nature to experienced seamen, and with it they have a foolproof method for standing on board without holding on, or continually having to counteract the tendency to overbalance. They are also left with their eyes and both hands completely free for work on deck. Anyone who has reached this stage is unlikely to suffer much more from seasickness.

Finally, seasickness can be deferred by suggestion. Here a distinction has to be drawn between auto-suggestion and hetero-suggestion. Auto-suggestion, which encourages an early appearance of the symptoms, is relatively common among apprehensive crew members. Early on they persuade themselves that they might be seasick and their thoughts continue to dwell on this prospect. The very first signs of the syndrome are then meticulously registered and anxiously monitored. People like this often react in precisely the way that will exacerbate their condition: they sit passively in some corner or other of the boat and resign themselves to their fate. It is possible to learn to combat this kind of self-suggesting and debilitating thought process. When the thoughts occur one puts a stop to them with a strong signal which has been decided on in advance. One breaks the chain of thought with a sentence to boost one's confidence along the lines of: 'This time I'm going to get through the trip without being seasick.' After this, the best thing to do is to engross oneself in an activity that occupies the mind with other thoughts.

Hetero-suggestion can also be quite powerful, as when, for example, the crew continually recall the possibility of individuals going down with seasickness with remarks such as: 'The last time we set sail with an ebbing tide and in a Force 5, three-quarters of the crew were seasick.' To avoid the effects of hetero-suggestion the skipper should make sure that seasickness is not the constant topic of conversation on board. If, when the subject is raised, he mumbles gruffly into his beard: 'No-one has ever been really seasick on my boat', he may well succeed in preventing some delicate member of the crew taking his symptoms too seriously and keep him from simply succumbing to the sensations.

The recommendations made in this section regarding the psychological approaches to motion sickness certainly cannot prevent it occurring when taken each in themselves (although their beneficial tendencies have been scientifically proven). However, a combination of the various psychological techniques which are appropriate to the situation may at least prevent discomfort occurring in a gentle swell, or, in the event of stronger motion stimului, ensure that the symptoms remain weak and are soon quashed. The advantage of psychological techniques lies in the fact that they are also still practicable when it is already too late for medicine, namely, when motion sickness has already taken hold.

When we have acquired our sea-legs

It is common knowledge that well travelled seamen no longer become seasick even though they may well have been ill when they first went to sea. The human organism gets used to the motion of the sea. This adaption does not take place in the appropriate sensory organs but in the brain. If the conflict between the information from the visual and from the vestibular system lasts for a long time, a slow programme change takes place in the brain which resolves the conflict by establishing the divergence as the new norm. This kind of reorganization of the combined and complimentary information from the senses has been well researched in psychology. There have been experiments in which subjects have worn reversal glasses over a continuous period which caused the surrounding world to turn upside down visually, while it obviously kept its original orientation as far as the sense of touch was concerned. In these experiments it was found that after 10 to 15 days the visual world was reorganized again, in other words, it appeared the right way up and consequently was once more in agreement with the information provided by the other senses. Typically there is an after-effect: when the glasses are removed the world is suddenly upside down again and it takes a few days for it to regain its 'normal' orientation. As previously mentioned, something similar happens after we have become accustomed to the motion of the boat: back on dry land we suddenly feel the after sensation of swaying as if the brain were still running the programme to compensate for the movement of the boat.

Adaption to the motion of a boat takes place on longer cruises after two to three days. Anyone who has not been seasick by then is unlikely to become so later. Those who have been seasick are, generally speaking, now past this stage of being ill. Unfortunately this is not true for everyone. With those who are for physiological reasons particularly prone to seasickness, the process of accustomization is retarded and, in extreme cases, does not take place at all. I have known crew members who were seasick for over ten days but who managed to get through it because they knew that in the end they would, like the others, adapt to the conditions at sea.

The after-effects of the adaption can still be felt two or three days after the cruise. It is, however, still effective for six to ten weeks, which means that on another cruise beginning within this time span one does not have to go through the adaption process again and one will therefore not become seasick again either. This explains why many yachtsmen are seasick once a year, on the first cruise of the season, and are then 'immune' for the rest of the summer and autumn.

It is interesting to note that adaption initially only occurs with regard to the specific motion of a particular boat. If the proud owner of a new yacht finds himself feeling seasick on his maiden voyage it is because he has not yet become used to the movements of the new boat. I have also known an experienced naval man to number among the first to report sick the first time he took part in a cruise on a sailing yacht.

Fortunately experience of different boats and their differing motions (and different environs as well) generalises in the course of one's life so that yachtsmen and professional seamen with many years of experience at sea generally no longer have to fear motion sickness.

Some advice in summing up

What follows is a summary of the psychological codes of conduct expounded in this chapter. Individual points, therefore, are not substantiated for a second time. Many of the codes of conduct may be combined, others are inconsistent with each other. It is up to the individual, according to his appraisal of the overall situation and the stage of seasickness, to find out which course of action is the best for him.

- Try not to think about seasickness, put it out of your mind, force yourself to think of other things
- Take heart and build up your confidence
- Practise releasing the tension in your muscles; as soon as you begin to feel apprehensive try and relax (desensitisation)
- Avoid unpleasant smells (especially tobacco, damp clothing, and vomit). Stay away from the galley
- Below deck: lie down, keep your eyes closed
- In the saloon: fix your eyes on a freely suspended object
- Seek out cool, fresh air and take calm, deep breaths
- Where possible keep away from enclosed spaces, go up on deck
- Reduce the amplitude of the motion stimuli: keep amidships or astern, avoid the fo'c'sle berth
- Try not to sit and let yourself be rocked passively back and forth with the motion of the boat
- When standing, avoid leaning against anything, stand erect and make active compensatory movements to keep your balance
- Try to move your head as little as possible
- 'Lock' onto the horizon; take the look-out duty
- Watch the swell and anticipate the movement of the waves
- Participate in the normal duties on board
- Take the helm
- At all events see a job through to the end, do not give up on it
- Get through a bout of seasickness actively. This speeds up the process of readaption.

3 *Recreational sailing as hard work*

Considerations of work psychology in a leisure sport

That sailing as a leisure activity should have anything to do with work, which is just what we want to get away from on holiday, may at first glance seem surprising. Under no circumstances, however, should work be equated with hard toil and tedium as is often the case with paid employment (and here it is immaterial whether we mean seamanship as a paid professional activity or are simply talking about the general characteristics of work). While it is true that one may expect to come under a certain amount of pressure at work it is also true that the working situation affords one the opportunity to test and develop one's skills. From this arises a personal satisfaction that only comes with the sense of achievement. Another aspect to consider, which has particular relevance to the situation at sea, is the co-operative nature of work. At work a special kind of social interaction is entered into, on the basis of which mutual understandings and friendships develop. For the above reasons work is considered by many psychologists today to be the most important factor in life-long personality development.

In order for all the crew to benefit from such positive effects while working at sea it is necessary to give some thought to the pressures accompanying tasks and to the organization and division of labour. Overtaxing crew members not only leads to unrest but also increases the likelihood of mistakes. Similarly, members of the crew who have too little to do or who always do the same thing are also liable to become discontented and lacking in motivation. The socio-psychological problems of work organisation are discussed in the following section.

Everyone has a job to do but no-one is satisfied – dos and don'ts in the division of labour on board

When an average club crew congregate for the annual summer Baltic cruise round Zeeland it is not long before the boat becomes a hive of activity. If one looks closer, it appears that each member of the crew has found a task which meets his qualifications and which he enjoys. The keen young dinghy sailor stands at the fo'c'sle and sees to the sail wardrobe, checking the run of the halyards and sheets and the sails themselves for possible tears; the motor mechanic busies himself with the engine, carries out an oil change and checks the compression; someone else looks after the anchor equipment, ensures that the windlass is operational and familiarises himself with the anchor fittings; another member of the party, having bought all the provisions, hurries to stow them away below deck and to draw up an appropriate checklist; meanwhile both watch leaders stand in the navigation corner bent over a chart and discuss navigational problems in connection with the forthcoming weather conditions; a further member of the crew, an electrician by profession, busies himself with the batteries and checks the voltage of the VHF transmitter with his gauge; last but not least, the skipper stands musing on the after-deck, inwardly debating the correct flags to fly.

This automatic division of labour appears at first glance to make good sense – everyone according to their wishes and capabilities. It only becomes problematic when, after ten days, the same distribution of labour is still in force. In the meantime discontent is sure to have reared its ugly head on board. The sailors who are called on deck, day and night, in all weathers, to see to every manoeuvre, complain about the 'technicians' who will not take the dogwatch because just yesterday they spent two and a half hours repairing the automatic bilge pump. These technicians in turn complain about the watch leaders who never explain the instructions they issue. The anchor specialist sits sulking in the cockpit because, on average, he is only getting a look in every two days when they drop anchor and because he always feels somewhat superfluous to the other activities on board. And all the ship's cook (who originally had only been prepared to shop for the provisions) knows of the Baltic is what he has seen from the perspective of the galley. He was the only one who was sufficiently well acquainted with the supplies to be able to respond quickly to the demands for food.

Something similar can often be seen with typical 'family crews'. Dad spends the whole cruise at the chart table, Mum stands to the left of him in the galley attending to the needs of the family day in, day out, while the two children are allowed, on father's instruction, to trim the sails and take the helm. Only when the harbour entrance comes in sight does Dad, gently but firmly, take the tiller from their hands. Even Mum is now given new tasks; she may make clear the bow and stern lines and place the fenders over the rail. It is just the same year after year, and then the head of the family wonders why his wife no longer has any real enthusiasm for sailing and wants to spend the next holiday at a beachside hotel in the Mediterranean (full board of course!). And the children, who in the meantime have grown up, go their seperate ways – on land; being forced to go sailing every summer when they were younger has taken its toll.

Psychologists have been researching and unravelling the causes of such discontent as it appears in working life for a long time: tasks which are too narrowly restricted, too little overview of one's work as a whole, the same thing day after day, year after year. These are typical characteristics of those work places in which a paypacket is the sole motivation. Motivation afforded by an interest in the end product or in the activity itself and in the contribution one is making to society is not found in these cases. The concept of 'alienation' has become a slogan for this kind of working situation. As we have seen from the situations described above the same thing can happen at sea. Just when people are actually trying to escape the monotony of everyday working life, they often find themselves, more or less unconsciously, experiencing a similar specialization and 'one-sidedness' to that found at work.

Such specializations, however, are not always entirely spontaneous in their development. In offshore racing it occasionally happens that the ship's owner or captain actually encourages them. The skipper of the racing yacht *Flyer* for instance, before the last Whitbread Round the World Race, is supposed to have put one of the foredeck crew in his place with the laconic remark: 'This is the port winch, your job for next year.' Experience of this kind of unfair division of labour in offshore racing must surely have led the race officials of the above event to include in the safety regulations the rule which states that winches must not be operated from stations below deck. A skipper's ambition and his disregard for others could otherwise all too easily lead to members of the crew spending the whole regatta as workhorses below deck – an idea which cannot help but call to mind the working conditions of the ancient galley slaves.

As we have seen from the examples, inconsiderate division of labour can bring the motivation to go sailing to absolute rock bottom. Under these circumstances sailing is neither a successful leisure activity nor even an opportunity for increasing one's skills or developing one's personality. And yet, in our highly mechanized and continually more complicated world, a sailing boat is one of the last reserves for real, all-round – and as they are often termed – 'social' skills. If one disregards the complex electronics on board to do with such as radar, hyperbolic systems or navigation satellites, all the skills connected with sailing are relatively easy to comprehend and acquire without the crew having to be engineers, mathematicians, physicists or even psychologists. A complete understanding of the procedures on board is absolutely essential, since in the event of difficulty far from shore measures still have to be taken: repairs carried out, calculations made (without a home computer), and personal conflicts resolved. Herein lies the very quality which makes sailing so special – on board we find our own relatively isolated little world, in which all problems that arise have to be solved with the means available on the boat which, generally speaking, means without help from the outside world.

In this connection every single member of the crew has the opportunity on a cruise to gain a comprehensive knowledge of this world in miniature and in so doing, by virtue of the clear parallels that exist with the real world, to gain the confidence in his own abilities which will help him to cope with more complex issues on land. Sailing, then, facilitates practical experience in aerodynamics, meteorology, mechanical engineering, mathematics, metalwork, woodwork, work with synthetics, radio operation, rigging, cooking, mechanics, first aid and conflict psychology. The opportunity to learn new disciplines is less a matter of taking home a 'diploma' after the trip than of acquiring self-confidence, being able to cope with new tasks not encountered before, and solving problems. The training in self-sufficiency and self-confidence through a realistic appraisal of one's own abilities, which is possible on board a yacht, is one of the reasons why more and more groups and associations have in recent years discovered the educational and therapeutic value of sailing for problem youngsters and generally educationally handicapped young people.

The fact that sailing can assist in personality development and in the development of physical and mental skills is an obvious reason why the division of labour on board should not be too rigid and, in particular, why the combination of the different activities should be easily comprehensible to every member of the crew. A taciturn skipper who after many hours of sailing with a free wind suddenly decides to change course without explaining the navigational considerations behind his decision is not likely to help his crew gain the comprehensive knowledge which they need in order to see their own actions in the overall context. A distribution of tasks on board which makes no allowance for the wishes of the individual crew member is also not desirable. A prerequisite for self-sufficiency is the ability to comprehend the context of one's actions, and the mastering of a nautical task can be the first step towards achieving this. Another requirement is that one should be self-motivated rather than externally compelled (by an order, threat, or promise of reward).

Anarchy on board is not the way to achieve a more flexible division of labour. Clearly not everyone who feels like it can set himself up as skipper; similarly it is impractical to have a different person in charge of the finances every day; it would obviously be dangerous if everyone were left to do as they pleased during safety manoeuvres (man-overboard or similar). A clear division of labour is nowhere more necessary than when formulating safety procedures on board. But in everyday life at sea, in ordinary manoeuvres under normal conditions, and in routine navigation (when it is not a question of negotiating a harbour entrance in fog), a flexible division of labour is quite feasible and means not only a considerable improvement in the morale on board but also that the crew learn more and are therefore better equipped for emergencies.

In work psychology a series of techniques for flexible division of labour has recently been developed, the so-called 'Flexible Working Practices' which, since they operate under the restrictive conditions of industrial units, are also applicable to the situation on board.

(a) Job rotation: the problem of boredom and lack of variation in a job can be reduced if several members of the crew interchange jobs with each other. This doesn't alter the range of individual jobs. The principle can be put into effect on most yachts if the galley duty is rotated among the crew. It only constitutes a genuine job rotation, however, if a large number of the tasks on board are included.

(b)　Job enlargement: in this case the individual task is broadened as various hitherto separate jobs are combined. An engineer, for example, would not undertake the inspection and maintenance of the engine for the duration of the cruise but would merely co-ordinate these tasks; monitoring and supervising the engine (when motoring for instance) would be the responsibility of the members of the crew on watch. Another example would be if each watch were given the job of checking the condition of the running gear and the sail while on duty. In one of their subsequent free periods the same crew members would also have to carry out necessary splicing work or repairs to the bolt-ropes.

(c)　Job enrichment: in contrast to job enlargement, which involves a horizontal breaking up of the divisions of labour by the inclusion of additional activities of a similar nature, job enrichment represents a vertical expansion of each individual crew member's scope for action. In this case each of the crew is generally given the task of establishing for himself what he is required to do and of monitoring his own performance and achievement. Whosoever's job it is to place the fenders between the quay wall and the side of the boat in the evening should also be responsible for checking their position when there is danger from the wind or several changes in water level during the night. Or whoever takes down the weather report should also (under supervision) draw up the weather chart and so on afterwards.

(d)　Part-autonomous work groups: this concept is the most far-reaching of the new forms of task formation. Part-autonomous work groups with a particular task to fulfil can decide for themselves how they want to work – where, when, with whom, with which methods, with what kind of labour division and according to which principle of leadership. It is true that as a model for doing away with fixed divisions of labour on board the extent to which this can be put into effect is very limited. A watch could certainly be treated as a part-autonomous work group of this kind; provided that the watch leaders are experienced and qualified navigators, a watch could seek to achieve their prescribed objective independently without having to go to the skipper every time a decision is to be made – when to tack, how close-hauled to sail, which sail to set and so on. This way members of the watch have a chance to do things on their own initiative and to learn from making their own mistakes and analysing them. Obviously the skipper should not hesitate to intervene in times of emergency if the safety of the boat or the crew is at stake. It is also true that while the autonomy of the watch is certainly a concept to be recommended on a holiday cruise, when racing, where everything depends on speed and on the exact calculation of the stress and strain of the materials (sails, rig, hull etc.), such a concept is less viable since in these circumstances it is essential that every unnecessary error is avoided.

In conclusion I have once more listed individual suggestions on how to avert frustration among the crew.

- Do not withold information – even members of the crew who do not initially know much about sailing still want to know what is going on and especially where they are going!
- Distribute and designate as many jobs co-operatively as possible – no one member of the crew, for instance, should ever have to stand peeling potatoes by himself for three hours at a time.
- The people who already know a bit about sailing should not think themselves above simple manual tasks.
- With unpopular activities in particular there should be a definite rota – the dishes, for example, should not simply be left standing after the meal until someone takes pity on them. This is usually the same person each time and he is guaranteed to blow his top sooner or later.
- To encourage motivation when allocating tasks, point out the interesting and educational aspects of the activity.
- Develop a rota or rotation for the unpopular as well as the popular tasks; do not allow a 'job monopoly' to form.
- Do not define a task too narrowly so that it appears insoluble out of context.
- Combine unpopular, tedious jobs with more popular, responsible tasks.
- Allow work groups (for instance, the watches) a degree of autonomy in setting their objectives and in the organisation and implementation of their activities.

On watch

While for the professional seaman life on board has from time immemorial followed a pattern imposed by watch duty, for the yachtsman watches are only kept on longer voyages, with large crews, or when sailing at night. Nevertheless the pure 'pleasure principle', according to which everyone on board contributes if and when they feel like it, is not always such a good idea either since responsibilities remain unclear. Certainly in recreational sailing we do not need to take watch arrangements so seriously that we are not able to organise brief, spur-of-the-moment spells of relief for individuals. When we are setting the watch on yachts – and this is absolutely essential in night sailing – we should not apply a rigid scheme but proceed in accordance with the different sleep requirements and fluctuating performance level of the crew over the period in question.

Everyone will surely already be aware of how their concentration, performance and sleep requirements are subject to variation at different times. Figure 36 shows a typical graph of human performance levels over a twenty-four-hour period. The graph was calculated from a large number of performance errors which occurred at various times of day in an industrial plant. The lower the performance level the more mistakes were made. The curve shows that performance is low in the period between 0000 and 0500hrs with a minimum at 0300hrs. It reaches its peak at 0700hrs. From then on on it slowly falls off for the rest of the day. A sharp drop takes place during the lunch period between 1100 and 1600hrs. If physiological functions such as pulse rate and body temperature are measured throughout the day an identical graph emerges, the only difference being that with body temperature there is no lunchtime drop.

Yachtsmen should definitely take this performance curve into account when they are drawing up the watch list. Unlike professional seamen, recreational sailors who only ever spend a few weeks of the year at sea are not used to a steady watch rhythm, and subsequently have difficulties getting through the night watches – especially the dogwatch between 0000 and 0400hrs.

Figure 37 suggests several possible watch plans. There are naturally a great many different possibilities which cannot all be cited here. The table is intended for long-term cruises and is based on the assumption that relief will always take place on the hour and, on successive days, at the same time of day; that is to say, there will

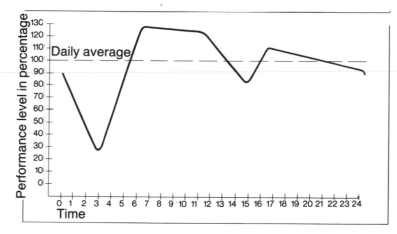

Figure 36. Fluctuation in performance during the course of a day.

always be a watch relief at 2400hrs at which point the watch schedule for the next day begins. It also presupposes that the watch duty is divided by three.

Divisions into two or four, however, are easily derivable from the plan.

On the left hand side of the diagram there are three columns. The first indicates whether each watch duty is to comprise of the same number of hours in any 24 hour period (hrs. = or ≠). The next column states whether it is a 'fixed' or 'rotational' watch plan (f/r). With a fixed plan each member of the crew takes his watch at the same time each day and with a rotational plan the watch times change from day to day. With watch periods of an unequal number of hours in a day, after three days at sea the same number of hours are worked. Finally in the last column (PC) the plus or minus denotes whether the performance curve has been taken into account.

Watch plan No. 2 demonstrates the four hour cycle which is customary in professional seafaring and which is indicated by a ship's chronometer. It is argued that 8 hour watches are better since they allow longer periods of rest (No. 1). Apart from No. 4 (regular 3 hour watch rhythm) all the other watch plans take account of the performance curve so that shorter watches are scheduled for times of low performance and longer ones for periods when we are more alert.

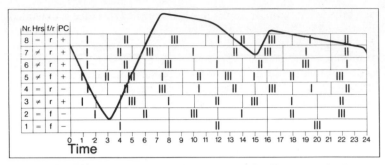

Figure 37.   The advantages and disadvantages of different watch plans (see text).

No. 8 is also an example of how the same number of hours can be achieved each day for each of the three watches with a rotating watch plan. Watch plan No. 3 has similar characteristics when the watch is divided in two.

It is also perfectly feasible to have partial relief during the night so that, half-way through their spell, half the watch are replaced by well-rested members of the next watch. Even with well-rested crew, however, during the dogwatch the level of concentration drops on account of adaption to the circadian (day/night) rhythm.

On long voyages in a westerly or easterly direction allowances should be made for the fact that the human organism adapts very slowly to the continuous change in time zones. One should generally allow 10 days for adaption to the change in local time. On these cruises the crew has sufficient time to devise even more complex watch plans.

Initial shock – reaction or reflection?

At sea one is often required to react quickly. Even more important than the speed of one's reactions, however, is their appropriateness. Since all traffic at sea – compared with traffic on the roads and in the air – is relatively slow, the importance of the initial seconds of shock in seafaring is relatively slight. Even when things happen unexpectedly there is generally still a few seconds time in which, by thinking quickly and weighing up the different alternatives, the correct response can be made. While on the roads a seconds' delay in braking at a speed of 100km/hr means that the stopping distance is extended by about 28m, the same time delay with a yacht travelling at 6 knots results in an increase of just 3m. The First Officer of the *Titanic* panicked at the sudden appearance of the iceberg and issued the order: 'Rudder hard-a-starboard, both engines full astern.' With just a few moments reflection this could have been modified into a more effective command with possibly less fatal consequences: either a change in course or as great a reduction in speed as possible.

But back to smaller craft and smaller problems. On board yachts reaction time plays an important part in the timekeeping operations which involve more than one member of crew. When two crewmen are trying to measure the altitude of a star for instance, the exact reading depends upon the response made by one to the signal given by the other. The same applies if one wants to take a taff rail log (trailing log). Between hearing the signalling call and pressing the stopwatch at least 0.2 secs elapses. This is the amount of time which is necessary for the acoustic stimulus to be collated by the brain and translated into muscular response. In certain circumstances the reaction time is even longer (up to a second). But even 0.2 secs with a measured distance of 6m and stopping time of 1.9 secs means a calculated speed of 5.8 knots instead of the actual 6.5 knots. It is generally true that, when the speed is logged in the latter fashion, the influence of reaction time means that the faster the boat travels and the shorter the measured distance, the greater the error that results.

Reaction time delays between two members of crew can be easily avoided if, in addition to the verbal message, one also arranges for a hand signal to be made. When the first member of crew begins to move his hand the timekeeper is able to anticipate the coming call and so react (by starting the stopwatch) with no delay. This kind of anticipatory response is possible if a signal has a visible course. The call on its own is in contrast an 'atomic' event. Delay through reaction time is unavoidable since response to such a signal can, in effect, only be made once it is over.

The question of how we normally react to situations first becomes a problem at sea when we are at the helm. Depending on the weight, lateral plan, drive and rudder type, each craft has its own special handling characteristics. Since boats move in a medium with low friction – water – the transmission of each steering movement is damped and consequently delayed. Thus, in order to bring a boat on course in good time, an anticipatory response which makes allowance for these handling characteristics is necessary. In a harbour manoeuvre, for instance, an incorrect rudder command is only recognised after a certain amount of time has elapsed and there will always be further delay before the mistake is rectified. In the meantime, however, a collision may already have occurred. Correct steering, in which the handling characteristics of the boat and additional factors such as wind and current are taken into account in advance is an art which must be learnt. Beginners do not, as a rule, allow for the yawing of the boat as indicated by the compass and, after a course correction, only take action when the head swings off again to the other side. This results in a snake-like course which, as is to be expected, means a considerable reduction in speed.

Figure 38 shows some of the typical ways in which helmsmen respond:

(a) shows delayed action – the helmsman responds with too gentle a movement of the wheel or tiller with the result that the centreline of the boat approaches the compass course too slowly.

(b) shows optimal action – the helmsman responds with a decisive movement of the wheel or tiller which is offset in good time so that the boat settles down on the compass course relatively quickly.

(c) shows a damped oscillation – after a rudder correction the boat initially swings off course again and is brought back by opposite rudder. This can result in a gentle weaving back and forth until the course of the boat is brought back into line with the compass heading.

(d) shows the typical behaviour of the beginner – namely an undamped oscillation; the centreline of the boat weaves back and forth in almost equal measure across the compass course with the result that it never settles down and the rudder bearings are put under a lot of stress by the continual course corrections. Failing to anticipate the boat's response is the typical cause of this kind of helming.

It is interesting and reassuring to know that the performance of seamen – in terms of accuracy and speed of reaction – improves in heavy weather; and this is true despite increasing lack of sleep. It is to our benefit that through the ages the exigencies of survival have meant that our attention span is increased in difficult and dangerous situations.

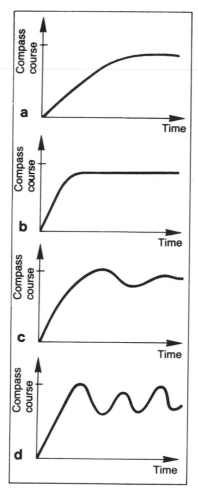

Figure 38. Various examples of steering behaviour – represented schematically (see text).

Safety at sea – not merely a question of technology but also of awareness

When the topic of conversation in the club or marina is that of safety, the discussion often amounts to no more than a simple enumeration of the technical safety equipment carried on board: life-jackets, life-belts, distress flares, pumping equipment, life-rafts, fire extinguishers, anchors, emergency steering equipment and whatever else belongs in this category. Even the safety guidelines of the cruiser division of the DSV (German Sailing Association) are essentially content simply to list necessary safety equipment. It is, however, easy to see that life-jackets carefully stowed in the locker seat or Very pistols hidden away below deck in the deepest locker do not really constitute a security factor per se. There is no need to stress the fact that safety devices alone, while necessary, do not constitute adequate safety coverage at sea. There are basically two things which must be added: regular practice in the use of the equipment and safety awareness, which is to be our central theme here.

An investigation carried out recently into accidents at sea revealed some amazing statistics regarding their causes. While this investigation was conducted in the realms of professional shipping, the basic trend of the results is applicable to yachting. In 14% of accidents natural phenomena are involved; the accident rate as a result of occurrences which are out of the ordinary (such as collision, fire, foundering) is 1%. Technical defects are the cause of around 4% and the rest, about 80% of all accidents, is put down to 'human error'. The last figure is certainly far too high. On the one hand this is because a certain 'insurance logic' frequently operates in the reporting of accidents which does not make clarification of the real causes any easier; on the other, human error is all too easily assumed to be to blame where the actual technical causes are not discernible because the equipment accords formally with the regulations. However even if we halve the percentage figure in which human error is taken to be the cause of an accident, it is still significant enough to warrant looking more closely into the psychology of safety at sea. As scientific research here is still very much in the early stages we are limited in this section to a few pointers only.

A lack of safety awareness and the resultant accident-prone behaviour can often be put down to irrational defensive reactions. Crew members consider it a sign of timidity to fasten their life-lines. Overlooking this safety measure is indeed falsely taken for a sign of courage and daring. It is often thoughtless skippers who directly provoke such behaviour: one regularly sees a skipper instructing his crew to don life-jackets and life-belts while not complying with his own directives. Unsafeguarded, he may even clamber intrepidly – and without a second's hesitation – into the rigging in order to clear a twisted halyard. Any skipper behaving in this way should not be surprised when other members of the crew, at the first opportunity, attempt to shine by acting in a similar dare-devil fashion. In psychology the process described above is called 'model learning'. The skipper, an acknowledged man of courage, is a particularly obvious candidate for imitation by those hoping to achieve similar recognition.

Another relevant aspect of safety at sea is habit formation. It could be said that bad habits constitute the greatest threat to safety. Anyone who has not made a principle of battening down the companionway hatch in a following wind is likely to have the safety of his boat jeopardized when a breaking wave suddenly crashes over the boat from abaft. It is a statistical characteristic of accidents that they occur rarely and unexpectedly. The only safeguard against them is for safety precautions *always* to be taken as a matter of course as and when the situation requires it. This kind of automatic habitual action is the basis for all safety awareness.

A number of both the smaller and the more serious accidents at sea result from misjudgements of the forces which influence parts of the rigging. Inexperienced sailors have, for the most part, no idea of the forces which actually effect a 50sq m sail when, for instance, they let go a sheet that has not been secured. It is even more difficult (for experienced sailors as well) to assess the forces acting on the whole rig. Here letting go of a backstay prematurely just once is enough to have fatal consequences. The problem with the more complicated rigs is that it is not obvious which forces are at work. Here only a knowledge of physics and as always, experience, can help. It is similarly difficult to judge momentum when manoeuvring larger vessels.

One very important factor of safety on board which has hitherto received too little attention is what I would like to describe as the 'user friendliness' of the equipment. Occasionally in a stressful situation where one is called upon to react quickly and correctly one fails to make the correct response simply because it is not obvious from the design of the equipment what this response should be. An example of this is the cut-off switch of a diesel motor which is not placed in a position where it can be easily seen and accessed. Mistakes also occur if one is unable to tell straight away whether the seacocks, valves etc. are open or shut.

The allowance safety devices make for the comfort of the user is another aspect of the user friendliness. The operation of safety equipment should always be as simple as possible. An interesting test in this respect can be carried out by anyone in a crew which is fitted out with different life-jackets; observe the times at which solid life-jackets and self-inflating life-jackets are put on and taken off. In my experience it has generally proved to be the case that the self-inflating life-jackets are donned sooner and removed later; solid life-jackets are furthermore more frequently undone or taken off completely when in certain circumstances they are found to be very cumbersome; an example being attempts to urinate overboard in heavy wind and swell. This very situation has resulted in many man-overboard manoeuvres before now. The fact that self-inflating life-jackets are considerably more comfortable thus has the result that they are worn more often and are often still on when critical situations arise. With the more expensive self-inflating life-jackets one is therefore also buying – from a psychological point of view – a great deal more safety. The clumsy nature of conventional solid life-jackets make them a false economy. Safety awareness is, then, partly dependent on the user friendliness of the safety equipment.

One final point in conclusion: the prerequisite for an effective development of safety measures to reduce human error is accurate documentation of all accidents, including so-called 'near-misses'. Unfortunately the majority of logbooks contain very little useable information on accidents. This is due on the one hand to the 'insurance logic' mentioned above and, on the other, to the fact that the importance of information gained from near misses in the prevention of actual accidents was, up until now, hardly recognised and certainly not acted upon in any systematic way.

Safety awareness, then, does not end with the obligatory installation of safety devices at the beginning of a cruise. The development of safety awareness at sea is an ongoing task for the skipper, the crew and, not least, for the designers of the equipment.

4 *The crew as a social group*
Socio-psychology on small vessels

The psychological situation at sea

When one reads sensationalized magazine articles with headings like 'Female Crew Members Murder Skipper' or 'Mutiny on Yacht – Two People Killed', one wonders how it is possible for such quintessential extremes of human nature to surface in the realms of a leisure sport. Why do we not hear of such things happening in motorcycling or ice-dancing? What is so special about the situation on board a yacht on a long cruise?

From a psychological point of view the situation on a yacht out at sea may be described as follows: the yachtsman finds himself for a long period of time in extremely cramped conditions with no personal privacy and with no possibility of escape. He is part of a group which has a fixed formal structure that does not necessarily coincide with its psychological structure.

In many respects the situation at sea does not differ in principle from the situation in a prison or cloister. Sociologists have described such living conditions as 'total institutions'. The lives of the members are completely bound up in the institution. There is no separation of the disparate areas of life which are found normally elsewhere: work, leisure and sleep. All activities are carried out within the same living space, with the same objective and under the same single authority – the ship's captain. The scope for communication is provided by the rest of the crew and, if one disregards the radio-telephone system, is restricted to them alone. Each part of the day and all the responsibilites are relatively fixed (watch division, safety procedures etc.). This description is characteristic of the Navy in the first instance, of the merchant marine in the second, and of yachting in only a small measure. But even in the latter case the psychological effects of living in a total institution must be noted.

As far as external, natural conditions are concerned, the yachtsman finds himself in an elemental situation, that is to say, all his activities are directly concerned with his survival. This gives rise to a special emphasis on action on board yachts. In contrast to other areas of life what matters here is not so much what a crew member says but, basically, what he knows and what he is physically capable of. Well travelled seamen develop the special personality traits which are useful in this environment and in this kind of social situation, such as reserve, caution, level-headedness and – in the positive sense of the word – deliberation. The psychological structure of the environmental situation on board, the social structure of the group and the personalities of its members stand in a dynamic developmental relationship to each other. In time a certain harmony develops between these conditioning factors. On the other hand there are the discordant demands that the yachtsman encounters in life ashore which influence his behaviour over the months leading up to his next cruise: ambition, stress, the necessity for quick reactions, the adoption of different roles and behaviour patterns in different groups, the need to meet deadlines, the need to be flexible about the place and time of work and the emphasis on vocal skills. These are just a few key-words which indicate that here two worlds stand in opposition to each other. Generally speaking, we grow up and develop in a world on land. When we go to sea we are 'socialized' for a second time. The change from life on land to life at sea entails special problems which will be discussed below. It might serve to shed some light on the matter if in what follows we analyse an incident which enthralled yachtsmen in 1982/3.

The Apollonia *case*

In the summer of 1981 two men meet in Pasito Blanco on Gran Canaria: one is Herbert Klein, a German businessman who has opted out of his bourgeois existence in order to build a new life for himself with a yacht chartering business in the Caribbean. To do this he has purchased the former flagship of the Bremen Sailing Club, the *Wappen von Bremen* and, after repair work and fitting out, has put to sea from Wesermundung in what is now the *Apollonia*. The other man, Paul Termann, was brought up in East Germany, trained as an electrician and after moving to West Germany became a helicopter pilot in the army and later a chief engineer with the Federal Railway. He has invested his life savings in a round-the-world cruise with his girlfriend Dorothea.

Klein has little sailing experience, he has the *A-Schein* (sailing certificate). For the stretch up to Gran Canaria, in addition to other crew, he has employed a skipper whom he dismisses along with the others on arrival in Gran Canaria. He has made several half-hearted attempts to learn the rudiments of navigation during this first stage. Termann has been sailing since he was ten years old. He possesses all the certificates and has travelled the first leg of his voyage on another boat as the navigator. Here in Gran Canaria his dream of sailing round the world is abruptly broken when he and his girlfriend are dismissed by the captain of the yacht *Orion* without their financial investment being returned.

The personalities of Klein and Termann, conditioned by their different histories, are dissimilar to say the least. Klein is regarded as a likeable person, he is amiable and fond of a joke. Carefree, frivolous, lacking in independence, seeking the good opinion of others; he both overestimates himself and is insecure at the same time. This characterization accords with the permanent holiday mood he has displayed since 'dropping out'. Diverse assessments of Termann on the other hand confirm that he was serious, reserved, civil, industrious, obliging, diligent and helpful – almost Prussian qualities of character – which occasionally develop into an insistence bordering on pedantry.

After the paths of Klein and Termann meet in Gran Canaria they become friends as they both realize how much they need each other: Klein has a yacht but no experience, Termann can navigate but has no boat. They are joined by two further members of crew found through a newspaper advertisement – Michael and Dieter. The crew of six, then, initially comprises three groups of two – Klein and his girlfriend Gabrielle, Termann and his girlfriend Dorothea, and Michael and Dieter. The members of the three groups have not been acquainted with one another beforehand. So when the lines are cast off for St Vincent across the Atlantic, the responsibilities on board are anything but clear and straightforward. As owner, Klein also claims the role of skipper, albeit somewhat half-heartedly. Before setting out he said that he actually attached no importance to it. Termann, who as the only one on board possessing the qualifications to command a vessel and who as the most experienced sailor is entitled to this role, accepts Klein's leadership to begin with since he believes in the assertive power of his professional expertise and navigational, technical and practical skills. No further role allocation takes place, but the frail hierarchy nevertheless begins to alter in the course of the trip. Klein begins increasingly to 'parade' the fact that he is the captain while Termann expresses his criticism of the decision-making or carelessness of the skipper more and more clearly. Termann insists on painstakingly accurate adherence to nautical practices and security measures. Klein is not at all particular about this for after all they aren't on the *Gorch Fock*. While the boat is travelling at full speed with the trade wind sails, the crew amuse themselves by jumping into the water off the bow and pulling themselves back in again on lines lowered from the stern. When Termann objects to this behaviour on safety grounds, he is derided as a coward. Klein and the rest of the crew deliberately set out to annoy Termann by continually knotting the running gear against his advice. In addition to the shifting tensions within the nautical hierarchy a group structure has meanwhile also been developing among this odd assortment. Klein and his girlfriend, together with Michael and Dieter, form a subgroup. They converse amongst themselves most of the time, they share the same attitude towards sailing, looking upon the Atlantic crossing as a holiday cruise. They sit opposite the other two, Termann and Dorothea, poking fun at them. Neither of the two subgroups can manage without the other, neither group can withdraw from the other completely. There are tensions between the groups which are sparked off by trivialities and which build up more and more in the course of the cruise. Offence is taken at insignificant details. The obvious thing to do had they been ashore, namely, to part company, is not possible here. Termann, for whom good seamanship and safety on board are the prime considerations, is constantly humiliated by Klein in front of the others. The social climate on board grows worse and worse with the tensions increasing to an unbearable level. The 'stronger' group around Klein celebrates the half-way stage across the Atlantic with a bottle of champagne. Termann and his girlfriend are not invited to participate. The crew are completely broken apart. Not even a 3 day storm rallies them. There is no longer any common purpose, no common goal, no standards and no overall binding hierarchy.

The frustrations which Termann has had to endure since the beginning of the cruise, indeed, since beforehand on the *Orion* as well, have brought him to a mental state where in his present position, from which there is no possibility of escape, they can only manifest themselves in either complete self effacement or extreme aggression.

What would under normal circumstances have been a trivial incident in this case lights the fuse to the powder keg. At the start of the morning watch at 0800 Dorothea prepares breakfast for herself and Termann, leaving the dishes from the night before unwashed. Klein is furious about this and a violent exchange of words takes place during which Termann announces that he is taking over command of the yacht and threatens to shoot Klein and his girlfriend. There are two guns on board. Termann and Klein each possess one. At gunpoint Termann forces Klein to hand over his weapon and demands that he write him a reference. Klein can at this moment only manage a grim smile in response to this provocation. Termann takes over command of the yacht in true mutinous fashion. Up until now Klein and the other members of his group have not realised the gravity of the situation. It is only now that they become fully aware of the danger they are in. It is clear that Termann's aggression has been accumulating from a vast number of lesser frustrations which were insignificant in themselves and which have not been considered important by the others. With the gun Termann is now the most powerful man on board. For him, especially in front of his girlfriend, there is no going back. For the group of four there is no way out. The socio-psychological situation is strained to breaking point, it will later be described by the survivors as having been a period of 'Psycho-terror'. Termann is now quite composed in the formulation of his death threat to the ship's owner and his girlfriend: 'You have only ten minutes left. I must first shoot the sun. Today, the thirteenth of December, is your day of reckoning.'

Fear spreads throughout the boat, irrationality takes hold. Klein offers to do the shooting himself. Termann humiliates him by giving him the opportunity to do so. Klein has to admit that he cannot do it. For the first time Klein and Gabrielle realise the hopelessness of their situation. On her knees Gabrielle begs Termann to spare their lives. Meanwhile, the others have gathered at the fo'c'sle preparing to tack and Klein urges his group to take action. The plan is to overpower Termann. Klein takes an iron pump handle and strikes Termann over the head from behind while he is sitting at the chart table. Termann reacts in blind rage and shoots at Michael and Gabrielle. Klein's girlfriend is killed. Dorothea points Klein out to Termann, who now has blood streaming down his face from the blows he has received. The third shot meets its mark and likewise proves fatal. With this Termann's aggression burns itself out. The corpses are thrown overboard. Termann composes an 'accident' report of the incident and merely threatens to have Michael and Dieter killed if they let the truth be known about what has happened – a feeble gesture in view of the fact that he and Dorothea intended to appropriate the *Apollonia* for themselves.

What followed was a matter for the courts and may be looked up in the case reports. Termann was finally sentenced to life imprisonment for murder. His girlfriend received a three year prison sentence for being an accessory. It was not only the court who were of the opinion that all this would never have happened on land.

From a socio-psychological point of view several danger areas present themselves for investigation on the evidence of the above incident. These not only determine the psychological environment during Atlantic crossings but on shorter trips as well: confinement and isolation, the group-dynamic situation, the role and style of leadership and the common causes of anxiety and aggression.

Social distancing – the problems of living space on board

If the *Apollonia* drama could never have played itself out in the same way on land, what then are the specific conditions which can arise (but which are obviously not inevitable) on board a yacht? In the first place, the 'social density' on board yachts is extremely high – there are often six to eight crew members living together for an extended period in 10 to 20sq m of floor space. This is the equivalent of an average living space of 2 to 3sq m per person.

Elsewhere similar spatial conditions are only to be found in overcrowded prisons. What is wrong with this is that everyone needs a certain amount of space to themselves, their own private area of responsibility and the opportunity to withdraw from others.

Even in the animal kingdom we observe that birds do not distribute themselves along telegraph wires haphazardly but spread out over the territory evenly with almost measured precision. Birds preserve a minimal social distance from their nearest neighbours which is maintained by one bird automatically leaving its place when another alights, and thus the system is self-regulating. People also need to maintain a minimal distance from each another. To begin with we each have our own personal 'buffer zone' around our bodies. The extent of this buffer zone, the boundaries of which no-one will cross voluntarily, is naturally dependent on sex, degree of intimacy with the other person and the nature of the situation. Invasion of the personal buffer zone is, of course, tolerated for a short while in certain situations; while waiting in large queues; in the cinema, and so forth. But even if one observes, for instance, tables in restaurants, libraries and so on filling up little by little, it is quite clear that people will always choose the greatest social distance possible in the given circumstances. The ideal distance between people is considered to be 1.20m to 1.50m. This naturally shrinks when common tasks demand a necessary proximity. On yachts the extent of the social distance, of the body's buffer zone in particular, is continually undercut due to the prevailing spatial conditions. Invasion of one's personal space has sometimes to be accepted for a considerable length of time.

Another aspect of spatial confinement on board is that everybody needs to define their own spatial and temporal area of privacy. There must, therefore, be a place for each member of the crew on board which guarantees this privacy and to which they can retreat as and when they feel like it. A sailor's bunk is naturally the most suitable spot. In the light of this care must be taken that on longer cruises every member of the crew has his own bunk and that no-one is allocated the emergency bunk which during the day doubles as the saloon seat. It is important that the private area of each crew member is respected, and thus preserved, by the rest of the crew. At all events, the absolute uppermost limit to the number of crew on a long-term cruise – and by a long-term cruise we mean being at sea for over a week – should be set by the number of fixed berths available. From the point of view of privacy, the space set aside on board for the individual acquires almost symbolic significance. The offer of a small locker, some place in which a few personal bits and pieces may be stored, will usually be gratefully appreciated by the crew.

Over and above the minimal spatial distance which makes the proximity of other people bearable, there is at sea – and in everyday life as well – yet another aspect to psychological space. The influence of this aspect on behaviour can also be observed in the animal kingdom: territorialism. Many species of animals have the innate tendency to define a particular area within their living space which no other animal of the same species (apart from their mate) is allowed to penetrate. The boundaries of such areas may be marked in a variety of ways, and another animal of the same species crossing them is met with aggression. This territorial behaviour is often a way of ensuring sufficient food supplies.

Territorial behaviour in people very rarely has the latter function. Rather it is used to define areas of influence and power or, at the very least, areas of responsibility. It is well known that people, according to their position in the social hierarchy, claim territories for themselves of different sizes. It is the same at sea. Traditionally the captain of the ship is given a cabin to himself provided, of course, there is such a thing as a single cabin on board. This is generally considered his due, regardless of his actual needs. Other members of the crew seek to stake out their territory in different ways. Individuals claim, more or less overtly, the galley, fo'c'sle, sail bags, anchor system, radio system etc. for their own personal areas of responsibility. This kind of territorial behaviour by human beings seems irrational even if, as suggested earlier, it does have deep roots in our evolutionary history. Generally speaking, it is an expression of undefined or unstructured power and authority relations on board.

Territorial behaviour may, in individual cases, take many different forms of expression. It can happen that a crew member feels his territory is being invaded when someone else takes over a job for which he has hitherto felt himself to be responsible. Such 'infringements' are always met with aggression, although whether this takes an open or hidden form depends on the position occupied by the aggressor in the order of rank on board. Some people manage to swallow their anger but this is rare. Another instance of territorial encroachment can be seen if the skipper constantly checks his watch leaders' navigation. This is an example of how the territories of the different role players on board can overlap. The watch leaders are responsible for navigation for the duration of their watch; the skipper, however, is at all times responsible for what happens on board over and above and including what the watch leaders do. Even so the skipper would do well only to check the navigation when it seems necessary from the point of view of safety, and he should do so as discreetly as possible. In any case the watch leaders learn best from their own mistakes, that is, when they have discovered the errors in their navigation for themselves. For this reason the skipper should only proffer criticism if it is requested. He should also always be sparing with praise.

Territorial behaviour of the kind described above invariably stirs up conflicts of authority and questions of competence. A skipper who silently demonstrates in all his actions how capable he is himself, and how incapable the others are, only succeeds in promoting the slow but systematic growth of dissatisfaction on board. How such behaviour can lead to serious socio-psychological tensions has been described in great detail in the travelogue of *Walross III*. Territorial conflicts are often an expression of other deeper rooted socio-psychological conflicts connected with group structures and individual power claims. This is why it frequently happens that seemingly trivial matters become the starting point for far-reaching conflicts as we have seen in the *Apollonia* case.

Let us depart once more from the detailed psychological structure of living space at sea and return to the general characterization of the situation on board as an area of increased social density. Here also we can learn by observing animals whose reactions arise simply because a certain critical social density (number of individuals per unit of space) is exceeded. Animals that are kept together under extremely cramped conditions react initially with increased aggression. They then retreat from social interaction. Their feeding and mating patterns are disrupted. Finally, with a further increase in density they become passive and die. The term given to the conditions of social density which give rise to these changes in behaviour is 'crowding'. It is nearly always accompanied by acute stress symptoms. Fortunately human beings are less likely to respond in the same way under conditions of crowding since they are much better able to adapt to different environmental conditions than most of the other animal species. Even so the human organism cannot endure exposure to the stress of crowding for long without some effects on behaviour. It often starts with one feeling physically ill at ease when others invade the already limited personal space. For example, two members of crew at the chart table looking over one's shoulder is enough to cause a very strong subjective feeling of claustrophobia. This also tends to lead to aggressive behaviour and irrational outbursts. If one feels claustrophobic in this way on land the normal reaction is to leave and go somewhere else. At sea this is just not possible. It is therefore important to take the symptoms of crowding seriously, whether one is aware of them in one's self or notices them in the behaviour of others. They should be made the object of a problem orientated group discussion, so that potential aggression is not allowed to build up into a situation which can have disastrous conseqences. Prolonged conditions of stress can make life unbearable, and stress through crowding can be reduced by taking the following measures:

- Clear role allocation and hierarchy on board
- Clearly structured conditions of interaction (who must be informed/consulted about what)
- Good social interaction
- Team spirit
- Co-operative attitude and co-operative activity
- Rational discussion of problems in place of emotional reaction
- Awareness of stress through crowding (knowing something is going to happen is often enough to reduce one's susceptibility)
- Closure of the bulkheads and passage ways from time to time to enable individuals or subgroups to withdraw
- Tell yourself that a restricted situation also has advantages which are often sought after on land.

The social density phenomenon of crowding on board can also be precluded during the planning stage of a cruise:

- Make sure the number of crew is not too large – everyone must have his own bunk
- Accustom yourself and the rest of the crew to social confinement beforehand or at least to the idea of it
- Concentrate the attention of the crew on the common task ahead and the problem of social density may fade into the background.

Social isolation at sea

As I mentioned earlier, to make matters worse one has not only to contend with a limited amount of space on board but with the problem of isolation as well. The isolation which prevents one from getting away, from turning to other things and from making other social contacts. It can, if it is the predominant feeling, lead to aggressive behaviour in itself (independent of social confinement). In this connection the triggering factor is certainly that the situation is felt by the individual to be outside his control – a restriction on his personal capacity for action which cannot be overcome by his own efforts. One feels helpless, as if hemmed in by inpenetrable prison walls. A consequence of this, besides increased aggression, can also be depression: a crew member in this condition becomes more and more reserved, melancholic and also more apathetic and less motivated. In the event of such isolation-related depression it is important to involve the afflicted crew member more actively in the activities on board, to entrust him with special tasks which are necessary to the well-being of the whole crew. The accompanying increase in his sense of responsibility serves to counteract his feeling of isolation.

Social isolation on yachts is, to a certain extent, closely linked with the problem of social density. It is, of course, a particular problem for lone seamen, be they single-handed yachtsmen or shipwreck victims. One important difference between these two categories however is that the single-handed yachtsman is much better able, through firm reliance on his own abilities, to endure social isolation than is his shipwrecked counterpart, who is at the mercy of the wind and tide. While the single-handed yachtsman always has the feeling of being in control of his craft and of reaching his destination by his own efforts, the occupant of a life-raft is controlled by the situation in which he finds himself and, as far as his being rescued is concerned, is largely dependent on chance. This is why in the latter case the feelings of despair and hopelessness take hold after only a short period of isolation. Even the most desperate situation is bearable, even for someone entirely on their own, provided they have some sense of having their position and environment under control. People who have gone through this kind of experience themselves have, therefore, been right to instigate the construction of life-rafts which are fitted with a sail and can be steered.

Social isolation can also occur in groups on long-term cruises, especially if the personalities of the crew are not compatible. Differing experience, seafaring ability and motivation can be sufficient grounds for crew members to so define their territories that the others keep out of their way as far as possible, and in this way everyone becomes isolated.

The social situation becomes even more difficult for individuals who, for whatever reason, are excluded from the social group. An important task for the skipper in his role as 'social-emotional leader' is to recognize this kind of isolation process in good time and to nip it in the bud. This is most easily achieved through a reorganization of the watches – within the new group the isolated individual often acquires a new social role.

The oceans are free – but we make territorial claims upon them

Territorial behaviour which links our instincts with those of our forefathers in the animal kingdom is not restricted to the confines of the boat. On the contrary our territorial claims all too often extend far beyond it. To begin with, many yachtsmen take extreme umbrage when, in an overcrowded marina, another yacht wishes to tie up alongside them. Excuses such as 'but we are planning to leave tomorrow morning at 0400 hrs' constitute the least aggravating response to a friendly request of this kind, since those boat owners who thus lay claim to the adjoining berth are often caught out next morning when they sleep in and the first face appears on deck at 0900 hrs. It is much worse when claims for compensation are threatened before even the first fender has touched the side of the inhospitable boat. What is insufferable, however, for the yachtsman arriving late, is to be forbidden passage across a boat by someone trying to defend his 'householder rights'. In cases like these it pays to inform the harbour master as it is he alone who has the final word regarding the berthing arrangements.

If, however, the skipper of a yacht which is lying in a raft is compelled to tolerate other yachts coming alongside him, as typically happens in a marina during the summer months, we frequently come across a kind of territorial behaviour already familiar from camp sites and allotments. Using bits of rope, a narrow passage is fenced off across the fo'c'sle which is supposed to discourage yachtsmen who are crossing from the far side to the pontoon from stepping the wrong way on deck. Since, however, traditional yachting practice stipulates that one should only cross the cockpit of a neighbouring yacht when it is absolutely necessary, this kind of compulsory barrier does not exactly constitute a sign of good sailing comradeship since it implies that neighbours would otherwise blunder through the cockpit.

It is not only the nations of the world that are extending their territorial claims more and more upon the open seas – previously 3 nautical miles, today mostly 12 and for the fishing industry 200 – but yachtsmen also seem, going by what one occasionally reads, to be considerably extending their territorial claims at sea. In the summer of 1983, for instance, there was a report about a motorboat by the name of *Beluga* which had anchored in the middle of the entrance to a Yugoslavian bay and which had put out land lines to either side, even though the weather was calm, so that other boats were denied access to the bay. The skipper of the *Beluga* ignored the requests of several other yachts to be allowed to pass, upholding his territorial claim to the 'private' bay. That such territorial behaviour in others – just as in the animal kingdom – is extremely likely to provoke aggression was illustrated shortly afterwards by the reaction of one reader who suggested forcing entry to the forbidden territory using a tackle knife and bolt cutter.

Group-dynamics on board

When the crew comes on board at the beginning of a holiday cruise they do not yet constitute a group but merely a collection of individuals. A period of mutual evaluation soon begins; of getting to know the attitudes and competence of the others while working together on board. Now and then something will happen to distinguish one crew member from the others. Before long the specific strengths and weaknesses of each become apparent.

As the chance collection of sailors gradually develops as a group, structures or well-ordered relationships also begin to form between individuals. These structures are in the first instance hierarchies. Someone is recognized as the skipper. However this does not necessarily mean that from the outset the latter occupies the foremost position in the psychological hierarchy. He must first prove his competence and superiority. Initially somebody quite different may be dominant; someone who has a friendly word for everyone, someone who in small ways makes himself popular and who consequently is the one the rest of the crew always look to first. The leader in the popularity stakes also tends to know most about the problems of the others since he is the one people confide in most easily. At the other end of the scale there may be a very quiet member of crew, someone who tries hard to establish contact with the others but who is quite seldom spoken to himself. In extreme cases he can become the 'outsider' who in the eyes of the others always does everything wrong and who should have been left behind. The outsider is, however, very important to the group and if he were not there his place would have to be filled by someone else. The formation of hierarchies in human groups is very reminiscent of something animal psychologists first noticed some sixty years ago when studying the behaviour of chickens: each bird stands in a particular order of rank with respect to the others. This rank can be ascertained by observing whether a chicken pecks or must accept being pecked by another. We come across this 'pecking order' in all human social groups as well – especially in the relatively isolated social groups at sea.

However, a group distinguishes itself from a simple collection of individuals by more than its pecking order. Members of a social group identify with each other; they pursue common goals, they share the same standards and codes of conduct and have the same ideals. The more closely integrated a group becomes the more strongly it stands apart from other groups, such as other crews.

Groups cannot be of an indiscriminate size. The optimum number of people is six. If a crew consists of twelve people, subgroups are sure to form, each with a hierarchy of its own and a strong sense of the common bond which sets it apart from the others. In the development of groups and subgroups it is found time and again that opinions, attitudes and standards soon converge and standardise. In this respect a single person can become the representative of different systems of values if, for example, he belongs to different groups at sea and ashore. It is important for the skipper to get to know as much as possible about the group structure on board. By taking account of the existing structures and skilfully allocating the tasks, watch divisions and so on, he should be able to avoid the discord which almost always has a negative effect on everyone on board and which is detrimental to the safety of the boat.

If so desired the group structure can be illustrated by a simple 'sociogram'. Each member of the crew is requested to write down on a piece of paper the names of the two other members of crew he would most like to form a watch with. From the 'votes' it is then very simple to construct a sociogram like that in Figure 39. Crew members are arranged in the plan according to the number of votes each has received. Each vote is represented by an arrow with a dotted line and each reciprocated vote by a double headed arrow with an unbroken line. In the illustrated case the results were as follows:

A chose C and D   D chose A and E   B chose C and E
E chose A and B   C chose A and E   F chose D and E

The sociogram in Figure 39 shows that E is clearly the most popular choice (he is the ship's cook); all the same the skipper, A, still has 3 votes. A shares a reciprocal vote with both watch leaders C and D. F is the outsider – he has not been voted for at all. The watches should by no means be organized according to sociograms like this in practice.

The nautical and seafaring ability of the crew should always be the decisive factor. However, the sociogram can be made the basis for an evening meeting in which relationships between crew members are discussed. This is a good way of clearing the air, of bringing problems out into the open which, once they have been made known, may also be resolved. No-one must labour under the false impression, however, that a sailing cruise is by any means a group-dynamic event. Sailing crews are, generally speaking, activity orientated groups in which relationships arise primarily through each member's competence and capacity for co-operation. Inter-personal relationships are initially secondary and only develop on the basis of joint activity. However if a crew really wants to pull together as a team then the problem of these relationships must not be ignored either. This is particularly important for racing crews. Well structured groups in which there are no subliminal interpersonal tensions perform considerably better than a collection of individualists and egoists. The advantage lies precisely in the aforementioned similarity of opinions and standards. It is this which forms the basis for mutual understanding, joint co-operation and agreement on objectives – not the pursuit of selfish interests. In this respect a collective evening to clarify where everyone stands in relation to everyone else is a must for a racing crew. For the holiday crew such socio-psychological exercises can be recommended as a means of ensuring greater contentment on board and preventing build-up of aggression.

A further aspect of group-dynamics on board, one which should be of particular interest to the skipper, concerns the preferred lines of communication. Figure 40 is a schematic representation of three very different communication structures which can and do occur in real life. In the Complete Structure everyone communicates on equal

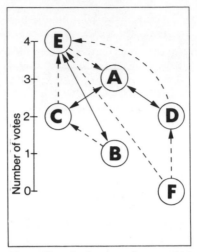

Figure 39. Sociogram of a crew (see text).

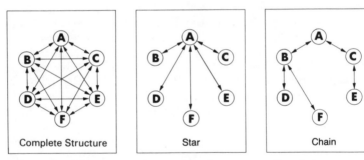

Figure 40. Three types of communication structure found at sea.

terms with everyone else. The skipper confers with each member of the crew and everyone is free to express his opinion without reserve. The skipper, A, is by no means the one to whom all verbal communications are addressed, rather every possible communication channel between crew members is realized.

With the Star we have something quite different. Here the skipper communicates with each member of his crew singly. The crew members individually do not know what has been discussed with the others.

Finally, with the third structure, the Chain, skipper A gives instructions or information to those next in line, the watch leaders (or equivalent), who in turn pass on the messages to the rest of the crew. Skipper A has, then, no direct contact at all with D, E or F.

Communication structures like these have been researched more thoroughly in social psychology with regard to situations other than sailing. It has been shown that the speed and accuracy with which information is conveyed in the Complete Structure is low and, by comparison, high in the Chain and Star. With the Complete Structure the leadership role of the skipper is relatively undefined. With the Chain, on the other hand, it is clearly emphasized and even more so in the Star. The crew are naturally happiest with the Complete Structure. With the Chain they are significantly less satisfied and with the Star, not at all. Even if, traditionally, different socio-psychological laws are accepted at sea than on land – the effectiveness of the ship's leadership in critical situations is always more highly valued than the contentment of the crew members – the skipper should nevertheless take time to assess critically his style of leadership and communication.

It is certainly true that with small crews on small craft a star shaped communication matrix is not necessarily optimal, nor is a hierarchial pattern such as the Chain model. On the other hand, the adoption of the Complete Structure for communications should not mean that each time a decision is to be taken it is first placed under discussion – making concerted action by the crew impossible. Communication between skipper and crew in the Complete Structure demands greater qualities of leadership, persuasive powers and expertise than the Star or Chain in which the leadership role of the skipper is already structurally guaranteed. But more on this topic in the following section.

What gives the skipper his authority? – on the socio-psychology of ship leadership

The skipper determines the 'working atmosphere' on board. His personality, conduct, the way in which he issues instructions – in short, his style of leadership – play a crucial role in determining the attitude of his crew. The general mood on board might be one of frustration and reluctance, with each member of the crew preferring to go his own way and only grudgingly accepting the division of labour. In contrast, it might be that the group works together as a team, looking upon each task as a necessary step towards the achievement of a common objective and refusing to become downcast in difficult situations. Certainly the skipper of a yacht is no longer the 'master over the life and death' of his crew that he used to be in the early days of seafaring, when he could uphold his authority by force of arms and was free to punish his crew in any way he saw fit. Nevertheless the responsibility of the Captain as recorded in the International Regulations for Preventing Collisions at Sea (4) imposes special duties upon him and at the same time grants him special rights. Co-operative command of a ship is in this respect out of the question. Of course this does not mean that the skipper cannot consult the watch leaders before he makes a decision or discuss plans for the cruise with his crew. In special cases however, particularly if the safety of the crew and the yacht are at stake, final responsibility rests with the skipper who must make his decisions clearly, unambiguously, promptly – and alone.

In the light of this it would seem sensible, in cases where several of the crew are taking part in an open-sea cruise for the first time, to discuss at a preliminary meeting not merely whether Becks beer or Budweiser should be bought but also the special socio-psychological implications that arise from having a clear leadership structure on board a boat. A student group would find it difficult, for example, to reconcile themselves to the idea of Mr X, someone who sat quietly in seminars contributing little to the discussion, suddenly assuming the role of skipper and being able self-assuredly to issue instructions to his fellows. Role conflicts of this kind arise because groups on land have a certain structure which accords with social hierarchy and in which emphasis is placed on communication skills. At sea the same group suddenly acquire a new formal structure because different skills and experience are required. These conflicts should be foreseen and openly discussed before a cruise. Otherwise the skipper's authority might only grudgingly be accepted, if at all, because neither he nor the rest of the crew are able to detach themselves from the group structure which operates ashore. It must be emphasized that while the idea of one person having formal authority is often regarded in a negative light on land (because there is seldom any call for leadership by a single person), at sea it can be the one factor that guarantees the safety and survival of the crew.

When I speak of the 'authority' of the skipper I do not intend to conjure up images of someone who no sooner has the deck beneath his feet than he begins to rant and rave, inflicting obscure demands upon his crew. I would rather we ask ourselves what the features are that distinguish a good skipper; how he may be recognised and how one should behave in order to qualify as such. Almost anyone who has sailed in different crews believes they know the personal qualities – besides seafaring and navigational skills – that make a good skipper. He distinguishes himself by his initiative, stamina, know-how, self-confidence, willingness to take responsibility, intelligence, sociability and so on. He is not an excitable type but exudes calm and confidence. He has a good sense of judgement and is physically fit. These are all qualities that skippers have. There are, however, any number of good skippers who lack many of them. Furthermore it is almost impossible to recognise many of these qualities beforehand on land. The positive abilities that a skipper possesses may only come to the fore in times of crisis. One need have no hesitation in saying that before now there was no such thing as the typical qualities of a skipper. However there are certain behavioural characteristics which are evident after only a short while at sea which distinguish good skippers.

- They are the most strict adherents to the group standards (eg: no smoking below deck, conscientious fulfilment of galley duty, observation of safety precautions)
- They do not sit aft in the cockpit issuing commands for the crew to carry out but participate fully, helping with difficult manoeuvres
- They do not take solitary decisions but, where possible, discuss in advance with the crew what is to be done, allowing them to choose from alternative courses of action or explaining the reasons behind a particular decision. When decisions have to be made immediately under pressure they discuss them with the crew afterwards
- They do not undertake themselves all the difficult tasks which require a high degree of skill (harbour manoeuvres, sail changes, sextant measurements) but, as far as the situation permits, give the crew the opportunity to learn and, in time, to apply and develop their own skills
- When a skipper issues instructions he must ensure that they are

well thought out and not immediately subject to amendments; they should be clear and easily understood. If they contradict earlier instructions, this should be remarked. Furthermore they should be directed at a specific person and the same person should not be given more than one set of instructions at a time ('Can you just clear the peak halyard and check the diesel')

• Finally, a good skipper is one who gets to know the individual needs, interests and problems of his crew and makes allowances for these in the division of labour on board.

This list of behavioural characteristics, although incomplete, nevertheless demonstrates that it is perhaps less a question of the inherent personal qualities that single someone out for the role of skipper than certain codes of conduct which can be summed up under the heading 'style of leadership' and which anyone can learn. In a classic socio-psychological investigation three different styles of leadership – the authoritarian, the democratic and the laissez-faire – were tried out in youth groups, each of which had a special task to fulfil. The authoritarian leader determined what and how things were to be done in every detail and only ever informed the group of the course of action one step at a time. He determined what each individual had to do and the group were left uninformed about future developments. Any praise or criticism was directed at individuals.

With the democratic style of leadership the method of approach was decided upon jointly through group discussions. Each step was planned jointly after the leader had put forward the various alternatives. The allocation of tasks was left up to the group. The group leader himself fitted in with the activities of the others. He praised and criticised individual actions, not individuals.

Finally, with the third group, all the decision making was left to the group itself. The leader did not participate at all and only offered his opinion when it was asked for. There was no praise or criticism.

The results of this investigation are very interesting and can give us valuable clues as to how to behave on board. Under the authoritarian style of leadership, a lot of aggression was apparent among the group members, especially against outsiders. Furthermore both toadying and power-seeking behaviour were in evidence. There was relatively little sense of team spirit and as the pressure diminished the group fell apart. Group satisfaction was low even though the task was completed relatively quickly and efficiently.

Under the democratic style there proved to be more independent work motivation among the group members. The group held together more and was satisfied with its activity, although in purely numerical terms its performance was not as good as that of the authoritarian-led group. There were, however, more original ideas produced by this group.

Lastly, the laissez-faire group demonstrated the lowest work performance and the least team spirit. At times there was no group structure at all, making the pursuit of common group objectives correspondingly difficult.

If we compare these styles of leadership and their results with the behavioural characteristics of good skippers which were listed earlier, the democratic approach would seem to be the optimal style of leadership. There should, however, be the reservation that in certain circumstances the skipper should exercise greater authority since it may be that such action is necessary to retrieve a difficult situation. I would describe the ideal style of leadership on board as 'responsible co-operative'.

Anarchistic laissez-faire leadership does not lend itself to seafaring. In our sociogram (Fig 39) we noticed that skipper A was not the most popular member of the crew. Crew member E, the cook, was most frequently named as the one with whom the others wished to form a watch. If we had asked different questions our sociogram would probably have been structured quite differently. If we were to ask 'Which member of the crew would you prefer to go on a pub crawl with?' it is highly likely that most of the votes would be for a different person than if we were to ask 'Which member of the crew would you choose to help you to weather a storm?' Social psychologists have found that in groups, and even in institutions and communities, there are two different leadership roles which are fulfilled by different people. On the one hand there is the efficient type whose qualifications and track record are undisputed, while on the other hand there is the popular type who is most likely to act as confidant for social and emotional problems. We enjoy working with the former and enjoy the company of the latter. One might think that the ideal skipper should combine both roles. However this is seldom the case because the types of behaviour determined by the different roles are, to a certain extent, mutually exclusive: a safety-conscious skipper who is concentrating on the task in hand may, in a moment of crisis, be unable to provide any social/emotional support.

An investigation which was carried out in the merchant marine shows that crew members consider those captains who possess at least as many social as technical skills to be the best (see Fig 41). The worst captains are seen, first and foremost, to be those who possess more technical than social skills, while in second place are those who possess social and technical skills in equal measure. It should not, however, be concluded from this that the position of a leader is best filled according to social skills. The most popular man on board may be the best skipper in the eyes of the crew but not necessarily the automatic choice when faced with a storm, in which case the most capable man proves to be the best choice. As the latter situation could be a matter of life and death for the entire crew, it would be unwise to choose a skipper for his popularity without due consideration being given to his seafaring and navigational skills. Popularity should only be the deciding factor when the choice is between two skippers of equal ability. In practice it is most often the case that the two roles are split in the manner referred to: the skipper being the most capable man on board and another member of the crew being the most popular. As analysis of reports of long-term cruises shows, this kind of group-dynamic situation generally proves to be stable and satisfactory. It only becomes problematic if the common ground and mutual respect of the role holders breaks down, in which case their personal motives conflict and the development of subgroups is set in motion. This situation can give rise to unbearable tensions. For a well-balanced group structure it is thus necessary for the skipper to accept the fact that he is not the most important person on board in every respect.

Another, often undesirable, role conflict on board can occur when the owner of the boat is not necessarily the most capable member of the crew. The owner can do one of two things: firstly he can hire a skipper – which may lead to discord later since, as a member of the crew, the owner is in the position of having to accept the skipper's authority and yet at any time he can make it clear to the skipper that he can be dismissed summarily. Secondly, however, if in order to avoid this split authority the owner claims the role of skipper for himself when there are more able people in the crew, then when it comes to a critical situation the conflict is even more surely pre-programmed. On board the *Apollonia* where this role conflict overlayed the rivalry between the most popular (Klein) and the most

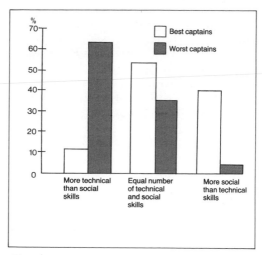

Figure 41. Captains judged by the crew.

able (Termann), the resulting socio-psychological situation led to the violent deaths of two people.

So much frustration – and then aggression

We have become acquainted in this chapter with a series of circumstances which can give rise to conspicuously aggressive behaviour at sea. These circumstances all serve to limit the scope and freedom of the individual; in particular, the cramped conditions on board, the few opportunities for solitary retreat and the social crowding which confronts the individual with the same people with the same behavioural patterns every day. Another factor is the unavoidable infringements on the individual's personal space which occur as a result of this kind of confinement and which we have defined as the problem of territorialism. Finally there is the question of isolation at sea and the impossibility of simply breaking away. Being becalmed for long periods with the accompanying inactivity and boredom can also bring morale on board to rock-bottom. In addition there are the problems that sometimes occur with the division of labour as described in chapter 3: too much specialisation, too little co-operative activity and, as a result of this, too little scope for acquiring new knowledge. Add an authoritarian style of leadership and the vat of discontent and frustration is full to overflowing. Aggression is the inevitable consequence. This may direct itself outwardly, but in most cases, in the absence of external objects, the powder keg of aggression explodes within the crew. It is this which at last prompts discussion among sailors in an attempt to resolve the situation by analyzing the problems one by one and working out possible solutions. Certainly not all the problems will be solved in this way, but even small alterations to the organization of life on board, avoiding provocative behaviour or even simply showing an understanding for an individual's problems, can help to lighten the mood again.

Not all of the potentially frustrating circumstances on board can be avoided: the amount of space available and the scope for retreat are determined by the ship's hull and there is similarly nothing one can do about being becalmed. However some of the other problems indicated here may be anticipated and, if discussed with the crew in the run up to the cruise, they may be averted before frustration and aggression have a chance to set in.

The recognition of what from a socio-psychological point of view are unfavourable conditions on board a yacht should not, however, outweigh the fact that year after year thousands of yachtsmen congregate in order to expose themselves to these very conditions for several weeks at a time. People are extremely adaptable, even to the most adverse circumstances, and there need not be any negative effect at all on the individual or the group from exposure to the environment on board and at sea provided it is voluntary. Even the far greater discomforts which the American aquanauts suffered for a period of several weeks in the underwater research capsule *Sealab II* – spatial confinement, crowding, darkness, the seclusion of the environment, being 20m under the sea and so on – did not lead to any group-dynamic or personal problems apart from the usual signs of stress customary under such extreme conditions. The capsule crew's co-operativeness and spirit of enterprise remained unimpaired for the duration of the project. Here too both civilian and military divers were voluntary participants in the venture. It is just the – fortunately rare – exceptions in which extreme environmental conditions on board boats lead to socio-psychological catastrophes like the *Apollonia* case.

5 What drives us at sea?

A word on the motivation of the sailor

The sailor and anxiety – producing action or immobility?

Every sailor certainly knows what it is to experience fear. By this we do not necessarily mean the fear one experiences in the face of a bad storm; there are many lesser anxieties such as whether the rigging and the sail will withstand a sudden squall; the anxiety experienced when steering for a harbour on the lee shore in a Force 6, or the worry about whether one will manage a harbour manoeuvre in the limited space available. Anxiety manifests itself in clearly perceptible physiological changes: one's blood pressure increases, the heart beat quickens, we begin to perspire. We call these physical symptoms 'activation'.

The sailor need not be embarrassed about feeling afraid. As long as fear is the response to actual danger it is a natural and even useful phenomenon. Sailors on the high seas are constantly confronted with the real dangers of their environment. Fear assists in the avoidance of danger. Fear in an ample (though not excessive) degree can mobilize forces which sharpen up the senses and improve one's capacity to anticipate and assess the risks inherent in certain situations. Our reactions are governed by rules similar to those we have observed before in other connections (see Fig. 26).

Figure 42 shows that with a low level of anxiety or activation our level of performance is likewise low. With a medium level on the other hand our performance is high. With increasing anxiety it drops once again. The optimum performance level is found with demanding tasks and a lesser degree of anxiety or with simple tasks and a greater degree of anxiety or activation. A very high degree of anxiety

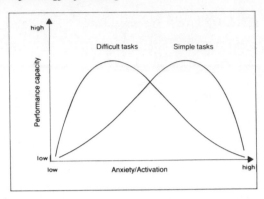

Figure 42. The relationship between anxiety and performance.

is generally accompanied by a steep decline in performance level.
More precisely this means that we suddenly no longer seem able to
manage the things we normally achieve effortlessly. A bowline tied
while we were under stress will suddenly fall apart because we did not
do it correctly. We also have to take perceptual limitations into
account: the green-red navigational light which marks the harbour
entrance is suddenly no longer distinguishable against the illuminated background of the port and even on close approach it is easily
confused with landmarks and buoys. We call this phenomenon form
disintegration (Gestaltzerfall).

Generally speaking a high degree of anxiety is accompanied by a
kind of constriction in our perceptual and thought processes. In
extreme cases we only see that which presents itself directly to the
centre of the eyes. The peripheral perceptions which are necessary
for a coherent picture of the surroundings cease to exist and we see
everything as if through a tunnel. Because of this distortions of the
size and distance of objects also occur. In the mind we have a stronger
sense of the present – we are preoccupied with the immediate
situation. We do not recall past events and we are no longer in a
position to anticipate future changes in the situation. This capacity is
reduced along with the attention span and the ability to concentrate.

How can we avoid the serious limitations to our physical
performance which are induced by fear/activation? One possibility is
by learning relaxation techniques similar to those we discussed in the
chapter on seasickness. Another is to struggle through anxious

situations and thus garner experience. It has been shown in several investigations into dangerous activities that experienced people feel less fear than inexperienced people. This is not because those with more experience have become insensitive to fear but rather because they do not suffer their anxieties at the same time as their inexperienced counterparts. It has been shown that seasoned sailors feel anxious some time before the onset of danger. Because of this they are in a better position to anticipate it and possibly avoid it. The experienced seaman can for instance foresee a spell of bad weather long in advance and is thus able to prepare himself and the boat to meet it and possibly even by-pass the worst of it. Even amid the dangers of a storm these people are only marginally afraid and are therefore optimally efficient. The inexperienced sailor on the other hand sails naively and blithely into the depths of a storm and is then paralysed with fear when it breaks about him. Experienced sailors, then, utilize the productive aspects of fear in advance and have learnt how to reduce anxiety in dangerous situations to an extent where their capacity for action and concentration is not impaired. This is what makes experience of open-sea sailing the best life insurance one can have at sea.

Why do yachtsmen insist time and again on risking danger at sea?

This is the question one invariably asks when one considers the loving and detailed preparation, the financial outlay and the anticipation with which yachtsmen plan the big cruise of the year. Fully aware of the dangers that may be in store, they surrender themselves to being tossed about in a small boat between mountainous waves which are several times the height of the freeboard, exposed to the wind and cold and spray; to being packed together with others in the most cramped conditions; to trying to determine their position with numb fingers and with great mental effort; to living out of cans – and all in the name of pleasure. To non-sailors it appears that yachtsmen invest ridiculous amounts in order to indulge in an activity for which they would demand hardship and danger money if they were engaged in it professionally. Even a hundred years ago experienced professional seamen would have considered anyone taking his life in his hands voluntarily, without economic compulsion and for purely sporting reasons, to be weak in the head. It is without doubt a phenomenon of this century, and of the latter decades in particular, that some people react against what is in many ways a sheltered, predictable and monotonous urban lifestyle and seek adventure, nature in the raw, the unpredictable and, to a certain extent, danger. There is no doubt that these people enjoy dangerous activities precisely because of the risk involved. They enjoy the flow of adrenalin and the feeling of superiority when they master a difficult situation through their own efforts. Little do they realise that from an insurance company's point of view there is a much greater statistical risk involved in taking a car on holiday on overcrowded motorways than in cruising at sea. The feeling of increased risk arises at sea from the direct confrontation with the forces of nature.

In the previous section we suggested some motives in answer to the puzzle of why some people, having taken to the sea once, go back to it time and again. There is motivation through curiosity – a desire in every human being to experience for himself novel, uncertain and unpredictable situations. There is also motivation through ambition -many monotonous jobs aford scant opportunity for satisfying man's deep-seated need to be constantly setting new goals, each one a little harder to attain than the last, and ultimately to feel a sense of achievement. Every yachtsman knows the feeling of deep contentment when after a long spell at sea he ties up in the marina. Finally there is the character-building aspect for which, again there is little scope in everyday life: the opportunity to develop further the skills that are required at sea where in the event of a problem one cannot call a craftsman or fetch a spare part from the shops but must apply one's own strength, brain-power and dexterity to the solution. When the cruise is over, the yachtsman takes the self-confidence that develops as a result of his efforts back with him to lighten the monotonies and frustrations of everyday life.

Index

Accustomisation 72f, 88
Activation cf. Anxiety
Activity, passivity 68ff, 113
Advantage to group performance 105
Aggression 92f, 98, 100, 103, 105, 113f
Anticipatory fear cf. Anxiety
Anxiety 67–69, 115, 116
Apparent movement 39–44
Apparent plumb line 60–65, 70
Atmospheric perspective 22, 38
Attention span 44f, 86, 116
Authority of the skipper 41, 81, 88, 91, 99, 106–113
Autogenous training 69
Autokinetic phenomena 39
Biological rhythms 55, 82, 84
Body position 60–65, 69
Brain 4, 65
Breaking the chain of thought 71
Brightness equalisation 33, 35
Causes of accidents 88
Cognitive maps 9, 11
Colour vision defects 36
Communication structures 106
Conditioned reflex 67
Conflict 98, 108, 112
Contrast 21, 32–36
Crowding cf. Social distancing
Depression 100
Desensitisation 69
Despair 100
Discontent 75, 98, 114
Division of labour 75–81, 104, 110, 114
Dog-curve 11–15, 16
Educational and therapeutic value of sailing 2, 78
Entenweg (the way a duck crosses a river) 13
Figure and ground 11–16
Frustration 81, 95, 108, 113
Gestaltzerfall (form disintegration) 116
Goal-orientated behaviour 14
Group discussion 100, 105
Group-dynamics 1, 103–107
Group standards 105, 109

Group structure 94
Hallucination 29
Handling characteristics of safety equipment 89
Helming 11, 69, 85
Homogeneous perceptual field 33
Human error 88, 90
Induced movement 41–44
Information flow 81, 90, 105, 109
Irradiation 35
Irrational defensive reactions 88
Job enlargement 80
Job enrichment 80
Job rotation 79
Kinetose cf. Seasickness
Land sickness 60, 73
Leadership roles 111
Location of sound sources 28–32
Lone sailor 100
Lookout 70
Loudness 36
Mind and body 1
Mixture of colours 36
Model learning 89
Moon horizon 35
Moon illusion 23, 42
Motion sickness cf. Seasickness
Motivation 77, 115–117
Movement parallax 21, 22
Neurotic illness 2
Optical illusions cf. Perceptual illusions
Order of rank 103, 108
Orientation 8–11, 60–65
Outsider 104
Part-autonomous workgroups 80
Perception of direction 8, 28–32, 60–65
Perception of distance 16–23, 28–32, 41–44, 116
of clouds 25
Perception of the horizon 31–36, 39, 63, 70
Perception of movement 7, 21, 39–44, 48–54, 65
Perception of size 16–23, 25, 116

Perception of the vertical cf. Apparent plumb line
Perceptual constancy 5, 16
Perceptual illusions 1, 5, 23–28, 38–44, 51
Perceptual laws 5, 22, 23, 41
  personal differences 5
  social determinedness 41
Perceptual restrictions 115
Perceptual thresholds 7, 22
Performance 82, 115
Personal buffer zone 97
Personality development 3, 75, 79, 92, 118
Personal space 96
Prägnanz 52
Preparation for the cruise 100, 107, 113
Pressure or stress 75, 92, 98, 115
Privacy 97
Psychological situation at sea 91, 96–100
Radar interpretation 48–54
Radar observation 2, 44, 44–54
Reaction time 85
Re-adaption 73
Reduced visibility 21–23, 29
Relative movement 41–44, 48–54
Role allocation 91, 94, 98, 111
Role conflicts 108, 112
Safety at sea 1, 79, 87–90
Satisfaction 107
Seafaring experience 89, 100
Seasickness 2, 57–74
  adaption 57, 72
  causes 65
  course 59
  duration 73
  medicinal influence 58
  psychological factors 58–74
  susceptibility 57, 59, 65
  symptoms 59

Sensory organs 4, 6, 60, 72
  adaptive capacity 8, 38
  the ear 28–32
  the eye 4, 17, 28, 40, 64
  hearing cf. the ear
  sense of balance 10, 40, 57, 60–65, 69
  sense of position 61, 65, 70
  sense of rotary motion 9, 40
  visual system cf. the eye
Ship, the, as a total institution 1, 91
Shock 84
Single-handed yachtsman 100
Skipper 102, 103, 107–112
  personal qualities 109
Social distancing 96–100, 114
Social isolation 100
'Social' skills 78
Sociogram 104, 111
Socio-psychology 75–81, 91–114
Spatial depth 16, 21
Spatial imagination 10
Speed 22, 47, 84
Stress cf. Pressure
Stroboscopic movement 41
Styles of leadership 109
Subjective contours 33
Suggestiveness 40, 54, 71
Sun horizon 34
Territorial behaviour 98, 102, 113
Texture-gradients 18–21, 25
Time evaluation 30, 54, 84
Vigilance cf. Attention span
Watch 44, 80, 82–84
Watch plans 84
Waterfall illusion 8
Weight-size illusion 27
Working atmosphere on board 107–113